Reading the Bible in the 21ˢᵗ Century

Roy Hanu Hart

 FriesenPress

Suite 300 - 990 Fort St
Victoria, BC, V8V 3K2
Canada

www.friesenpress.com

Cover design by Holly Moore (streamstrider@gmail.com).

ISBN
978-1-5255-3551-2 (Hardcover)
978-1-5255-3552-9 (Paperback)
978-1-5255-3553-6 (eBook)

1. Religion, Biblical Criticism & Interpretation

Distributed to the trade by The Ingram Book Company

To my grandfather Abraham,
who started me on the Great Journey when I was ten.

ACKNOWLEDGEMENTS

I usually begin my acknowledgements with philologist Dr. David Flusser, late Professor of Early Christianity and Judaism of the Second Temple Period at the Hebrew University of Jerusalem. His book *Jesus* (1965), drawn from many of the thousand articles he wrote in Hebrew, German, English, and other languages, served as my introduction to the study of Jesus of Nazareth four decades ago.

Flusser was co-founder of the Jerusalem School of Synoptic Research with Christian scholar Robert L. Lindsey in the 1960s. The Jerusalem School is "a consortium of Jewish and Christian scholars that study the Synoptic Gospels in light of the historic, linguistic and cultural milieu of Jesus." I have read the works of several members of the Jerusalem School, including David Bivin's New *Light on the Difficult Words of Jesus* and the earlier work he co-wrote with Roy Blizzard, Jr., *Understanding the Difficult Words of Jesus*, and I found both these books exceedingly helpful.

The Miracles of Exodus by the renowned Cambridge University scientist Colin Humphreys was my major source in writing about Moses in *Reading the* Bible *in the 21ˢᵗ Century* (RTB). Humphreys is a Fellow of the Royal Academy of Engineering, Fellow of the Institute of Physics, and a Fellow of the Institute of Materials. He uses his expertise in physics, chemistry, astronomy, and geology to pursue what we might refer to as a modern-day approach to the study of the Bible.

Without Julian Jaynes' *The Origin of Consciousness in the Breakdown of the Bicameral Mind*, I would not have been able to piece together a psychological portrait of Moses. Jaynes' theory of bicamerality is brilliant…and contentious. Whatever its merits and demerits, I find it utilitarian.

Rabbi Stephen M. Wylen's *The Jews in the Time of Jesus* was a helpful introduction to understanding the Jewish roots of Christianity, which I first read many years ago. Like Rabbi Wylen, I am fond of Hillel's saying that encourages us "to learn something new each day, because we are always moving either forwards or backwards."

Another scholar whose books helped me acquire a basic knowledge of Jesus of Nazareth was Bruce Chilton, formerly of Cambridge University and now Professor of Religion at Bard College in Upstate New York. I had occasion to read several of his works, including *Rabbi Jesus: An Intimate Biography*.

The Parables: Jewish Tradition and Christian Interpretation by Brad H. Young, one of David Flusser's proteges, was an invaluable source for an understanding of Jesus' use of parables.

With his essay "Moses," Ahad Ha-'Am (ne Asher Ginzberg), the founder of cultural Zionism, opened the way to a new branch of history. The world of scholarship is indebted to him.

Flusser, Bivin, Jaynes, Blizzard, Humphreys, Wylen, Young, Ginzberg, and Chilton are only some of the many scholars from whom I have drawn in writing RTB. I thank them all for contributing to my understanding of God's Book.

PREFACE

*R*eading the Bible in the 21ˢᵗ Century is based on a series of lectures I have given over the years, and the conversational tone of those talks will be evident as the reader proceeds through the book, which I like to think is reader-friendly. I usually began my lectures with a bit of levity: "I am not a historian, and what's even more incriminating, I have never played one on television."[1] I'm a psychiatrist, and I approach biblical theology and history with the tools of the psychodynamic psychiatrist and a background in literature.

During the Q&A following my lectures, I could always expect to be asked: "Do you believe the Bible is the word of God?" I responded by focusing on what the apostle Paul wrote in 2 Timothy 3:16: "All Scripture is God-inspired," and the even stronger Greek translation, "All Scripture is God-breathed." God's breath in Hebrew is *ruach*, and *Ruach haKodesh* is the Holy Spirit of God. The fundamentalists in the audience are never satisfied with either of my responses; so I go to another source. In a chapter entitled "What Does It Mean to Say the Bible Is the Word of God?" from *Did God Really Command Genocide?* authors Paul Copan and Matthew Flannagan write this about the relationship between divine and human authorship of Scripture: "God appropriates the human writers' work as his own speech, delegating the

---

1   A take-off on the television commercial, "I'm not a Doctor, but I play one on TV," first aired in 1984 on *General Hospital,* followed by a rash of copycats.

biblical authors to speak on his behalf. So the human writers' work becomes God's word to us...."

The material in chapter 2 dealing with contemporary social matters may seem out of place in a book about the Bible. It is included here to contrast the halcyon life of Adam and Eve in Eden (before the "apple affair") with the turbulence and stress in the lives of – and between – men and women in our postmodern world.

Let me illustrate this. "And the LORD God said, It is not good that the man should be alone; I will make him an help meet for him" (Genesis 2:18). A *help meet* for Adam implies more than simply a helper. Closer to the intent of the original Hebrew, the meaning is that of a helper who is his opposite half with opposite attributes.

Genesis 1:27 helps clarify matters for us: "So God created man in his own image,[2] in the image of God created he him; male and female created he them." Not only did God create humanity with Adam and Eve, but in the process, He placed some of His "attributes" within each: His male attributes in Adam and His female attributes in Eve. God created two sexes but one humanity.

Is what is going on today – the war between the sexes --part of God's plan for humanity, or are we going seriously astray? And what has all this to do with a book on the Bible, anyway? Genesis 1:27 is a bombshell. The detonation of the first atomic bomb on July 16, 1945, outside of Alamogordo, New Mexico, prompted J. Robert Oppenheimer, the "father of the atomic bomb," to utter these chilling words from the Bhagavad Gita: "Now I am become Death, the destroyer of worlds." Am I comparing the war between the sexes to a WMD? Certainly not. Then why such melodramatic

---

2   Not to be interpreted as an image seen in a mirror but fashioned from God's very attributes.

language? Well, I'm trying to call attention to the current interne-cine strife between the sexes, because if this bitter sexual warfare continues on its course, it will be our undoing as a species. Those who are part of Judeo-Christian America will most likely agree with what I write in chapter 2, while the other half of the country, which can be called secular, or pagan, America, won't.

Now for a couple of loose ends. In these pages, I quote liberally from the Bible, and all quotations are from the King James Version (KJV), unless otherwise indicated. My reasons for choosing the KJV are to be found in the opening paragraph of chapter 1 (and in the material below on gender-neutral language).

The Chicago Manual of Style and *The New York Times Manual of Style*, old writers' standbys, appear to be out of style in the post-modern era. Despite the lackadaisical approach to grammar and punctuation nowadays, I stick with as many of the grammatical rules I'm able to remember from grade-school days (which began for me in 1935). For one thing, I do not split the infinitive, and I will use Star Trek's famous opening to provide an illustration: "to boldly go where no man has gone before." In this example, "boldly" splits the infinitive. "To not be" is another no-no. Shakespeare got it right when he had Hamlet say: "To be or not to be."

Punctuation has become a tedious issue, but there are several rules we *used* to follow. For instance, following a prepositional phrase, such as "in this example" in the above paragraph, and in "in the above paragraph," I tack on a comma. That's one rule I remember. Paragraphing, however, no longer follows the old rules. It used to be taught that a paragraph should consist of five sentences: a topic sentence, three supporting sentences, and a concluding sentence. In this day and age of shrinking attention spans, the idea is to keep paragraphs as short as possible. (But there are times when you can't.)

Those readers familiar with my writings know only too well that I do not go in for gender-neutral language. To illustrate this point, the New International Version (NIV) translation of Numbers 12:6: "… When there is a prophet among you, I, the LORD, reveal myself to them in visions, I speak to them in dreams," rubs me the wrong way. I adhere to the translation in the King James Version (KJV): "And he said…If there be a prophet among you, I the LORD will make myself known unto him in a vision, and will speak unto him in a dream."

I prefer grammatical consistency and clarity. The rule in this instance calls for subject-object agreement. We don't have that in the NIV. Here's another grammatical absurdity from an ad for a product promoted by a well-known screen actor: "Check with a doctor first. They will be able to tell you.…" By "a doctor" is meant one doctor. "They" is a plural pronoun. The gender neutralists say "they" can also be singular. That won't do. There used to be grammatical rules… when schools taught English grammar.

Consider the definition of "cis-gender," courtesy of Google: "relating to a person whose sense of personal identity and gender correspond with their birth sex." In order to be grammatically consistent, "their" should be "his." That's the old rule.

You don't abandon subject-subject agreement in order to satisfy those who clamor for a degenderized world. Now, in 2018, we have reached a point where gender neutralization, that is to say, sexual neutralization, has become the number one issue of our time. It is the first topic dealt with in the book – from a biblical perspective.

No doubt the professionals in the field of Judeo-Christian studies will find this work seriously flawed, but no matter. Despite its imperfections, *Reading the Bible in the 21st Century* contains ideas that should challenge the experts and stimulate readers.

Roy Hanu Hart (Yitzhak Hanu)
June 1, 2018

CHAPTER 1

As of 2017, the Bible had been translated into 670 languages. The number of English translations and paraphrases of the Bible comes to about 900. According to the Nielsen ratings for 2016, the five most popular versions in English are: New International Version (NIV), King James Version (KJV), New Living Translation (NLT), English Standard Version (ESV), and New King James Version (NKJV). For my taste, or rather that of my central neuronal connections, it is the Elizabethan English of the King James translation, preserving as much as is possible of the wonderful metaphoric language and word flow of the Hebrew, along with the simplicity of language of the original, that makes the KJV my favorite translation of the Bible in English.

By way of illustration, in the late 1940s, CBS Radio broadcast a series, *You Are There*, recreating great events of the past. Imagine being there with Moses when "Pharaoh said, Who is the LORD, that I should obey his voice to let Israel go? I know not the LORD, neither will I let Israel go" (Exodus 5:2, KJV).

Compare that with the New Living Translation (NLT): "Is that so?" retorted Pharaoh. "And who is the LORD? Why should I listen to him and let Israel go? I don't know the LORD, and I will not let Israel go."

The latter translation is certainly easier on the modern ear, but the archaic language of the KJV heightens your sense of being there. You're not there with the NLT. You're on your couch, and it's 2018.

The Bible continues to be the best-selling book in the world: more than one hundred million copies are sold or given away free every year. The Bible,[3] of course, isn't a single book but a collection of books written by a number of authors covering more than fifteen hundred years of Jewish history. Some of the books are historical, others narratives, allegories, short stories, apocalyptic literature, epic tales, prophetic books, poetry....

Consider for a moment Adam and Eve, the progenitors of the human race, according to the Genesis account. Is the biblical narrative factual or something else? Religious fundamentalists, who view the Bible as both a history book as well as a theological book, take the story literally.

We may begin by asking where Adam and Eve belong in time. For the 17th-century Irish prelate James Ussher, October 23, 4004 B.C. marked the first day of creation, and young Earth creationists, heirs to Bishop Ussher, maintain that all creation happened less than 10,000 years ago. That would place Adam and Eve in the recent past. On the other hand, geochronologists calculate the age of our planet to be 4.6-billion years, and humans have been part of the landscape for 200,000 years, which I think most people will agree is not the recent past. The universe itself is approximately 13.8-billion years old. For the psalmist, "A thousand years in your sight are like a day" (Psalm 90.4). Actually, 2.3-billion years would be more like a day to God, who created all that is in 6 days, periods, epochs, intervals, cycles or stages. ("Epoch" and "period" are used here in their general sense. Geologically, we are living in the Holocene epoch, part of the Quaternary period, which began 11,700 years ago after the last major ice age.)

DNA testing reveals that the Sans (Bushmen) people of southern Africa are the oldest continuous population of humans. These hunter-gatherers, descendants of Early Stone Age ancestors, are

---

3   By the Bible, I should add I am speaking of the Hebrew Bible, which Christians call the Old Testament.

the closest people to the original *Homo sapiens* nucleus. If you must place the Garden of Eden somewhere, then the South African-Namibian border is as likely a location as any.

There are a number of ways to interpret the Adam and Eve narrative. Simply stated, Adam and Eve offer one explanation of why we are mortal and not immortal. God warned Adam not to eat of the fruit of the tree of the knowledge of good and evil, "for in the day that thou eatest thereof thou shalt surely die" (Gen. 2:17). Updating the matter, all living things die, and that's the way it has always been. The way life is organized on earth, everything that is alive eats something else that is alive or was alive, or is a product of something that is or was alive.

God is responsible for the laws of nature, and His second law of thermodynamics, in one non-mathematical formulation, states that heat flows from hot bodies to cold bodies (and never the other way), which means that in the end everything, including the universe itself, will die a cold death. Death, in other words, is inevitable, and this has always been a universal truth, except for biblical literalists.

The second law of thermodynamics, the entropy law, states that entropy, the level of disorder or randomness in a system, increases in every natural thermodynamic process. In terms of human activity, entropy is increasing. Life is a struggle against entropy – in order to create order out of disorder – which requires effort, self-discipline, and something our Founding Fathers considered essential: virtue, a non-thermodynamic concept.

Mortality/immortality is also the central theme in the *Epic of Gilgamesh*, the epic poem from ancient Mesopotamia considered the oldest surviving work of literature. The poem contains an account of a universal flood that bears remarkable similarities to the flood story in Genesis[4] with some minor differences: Noah's equivalent in the Babylonian version is Utnapishtim; Noah's boat is rectangular, Utnapishtim's, square; Noah's flood lasted 40 days and nights, Utnapishtim's, 6 days and nights; Noah released a raven and 3 doves on sighting land, Utnapishtim, a dove, swallow, and raven; and Noah landed on Mt. Ararat somewhere in north-eastern Turkey, Utnapishtim on Mt. Nisir near the modern city of Sulaymeniyah in Iraqi Kurdistan.

The story revolves around King Gilgamesh of Uruk in ancient Sumer and his close friend Enkidu, a "wild man" molded from water and clay by the creator of mankind, the goddess Aruru, and civilized by Shamhat, a sacred prostitute.[5] When Enkidu is killed, a distraught Gilgamesh goes on a quest to discover the secret of everlasting life. He seeks out Utnapishtim, who has survived the flood and has been granted immortality by the gods. What Gilgamesh learns is that when the gods created man, "they let death be his share."

In the *Myth of Adapa*, a 14th-century BCE Mesopotamian story, Adapa, also identified as Adamu, was endowed with wisdom but not everlasting life by his father, the god Ea, one of the three most powerful gods in the Mesopotamian pantheon. When offered immortality by Anu, the sky god and highest god, he is tricked and loses his chance to become one of the immortals.

Here's another angle on our legendary remote parents. "By the waters of Babylon, there we sat down and wept, when we remembered Zion" (Psalm 137:1), so sang (some of) the exiles in Babylon following Nebuchadnezzar's conquest of Judah in 586 BCE. Guilt,

---

4   Many cultures have ancient flood stories.

5   Interpretation: Woman civilizes man!

a Jewish invention,[6] by the way, is a negative emotion, but in the service of the ego, it can lead to a realization of one's sins. The Jews, cast out of the land flowing with milk and honey, realized their own fallen story in the story of Adam and Eve expelled from their paradisiacal garden in the land of Eden for their sinning – and may as a consequence have inspired the writing of the Adam and Eve story.

There is, of course, much more we can learn from Adam and Eve, who started life in the Womb of Eden. For instance, the difference between what is eternal and what is immortal. That which is eternal has never come into existence but has always been. What is immortal had a beginning. God, the Eternal One, had no beginning. He has always been. Thus, if the universe requires a creator, then the Eternal One is the likely Creator.

God alone is eternal. Adam and Eve may have been denied immortality, yet they are, paradoxically, *immortal*. They live on in the pages of the Bible, and they pop up now and then in discussions of various sorts. Moses, Alexander the Great, George Washington, Abraham Lincoln, Florence Nightingale, John Wayne are immortal. They live on in memory. The last mentioned may be on your television screen right now. Perform some deed that adds to the glory of God, and your name will be added to those of the immortals. What about Tolui Khan[7], Hitler, Tojo,[8] Stalin, Jack the Ripper, Al Capone, Ted Bundy? Their names may live on – but in infamy.

---

6   Hitler said that "conscience is a Jewish invention; it is a blemish like circumcision." Nazism condemned Judaism for having introduced ethics into history.

7   Fourth son of Genghis Khan, who slaughtered the entire population of Nishapur in northeastern Iran in 1221. Historians remember him well.

8   Hideki Tojo – prime minister of Japan during the greater part of World War II.

And then there are the personal meanings people find in reading Genesis. One lesson for me: Whatever is has its cause, which brings me to the watchmaker analogy, a teleological[9] argument for the existence of God. The argument simply states that a design implies the existence of a designer. Thus, if you come upon a watch partially buried in the sand while strolling along a beach, you can conclude that somewhere something, a designer, brought it into existence.

If instead of a watch, you find a Coca Cola bottle on that beach, you know it didn't materialize out of the ether. Somewhere there is a Coca Cola plant where employees fashioned it.

If you see a universe, look for its Designer. It may take you a while, perhaps a lifetime, but the exploration, or quest, if that be your odyssey, is worth it.

I see in Genesis a paean to God. It doesn't matter whether God created the world in six days, six epochs, or six whatever. What Genesis is telling us is that He saved His creation of man, the highest form of life anywhere in His domain, for last – His final act as the Creator. Whenever I finish reading the creation story in Genesis, and I reread it from time to time, I shout out: "*L'chaim!*" – "To life!" God is telling us: Laud it, love it, live it!

God was pleased with what He had created: "And God saw every thing he had made, and, behold, *it was* very good" (Gen. 1:31). "And God blessed them [Adam and Eve]" (Gen. 1:28) and gave them [the human race] dominion over the earth.

God chose one planet in the incomprehensible vastness of space to bless. For God, Earth and its human inhabitants are special, and He extols us to celebrate life: *L'chaim!*"

Judaism's focus is on *HaOlam Hazeh* ("this world"). *HaOlam Haba* ("the world to come") is part of Jewish eschatology, but the

---

9   Teleology: the doctrine of design and purpose in nature.

Hebrew Bible does not deal with the subject of the afterlife (*Olam Haba*). Compare Philippians 3:20 (NIV): "But our citizenship is in heaven...." For Christians, this life is only a preliminary to the next world, for those who satisfy the entrance qualifications, which is the true life.

At the Reverend Billy Graham's funeral, his son Franklin quoted "America's pastor" as having said: "I'm not afraid to die because I know the joys of heaven are waiting...We enter eternity when we die."The second part of the quote would be acceptable to most Jews. In death, we become re-united with the Eternal, who gave us life.

However, the Christian belief in an immortal soul is something that is not dealt with in the Hebrew Bible. Genesis 2:7 describes God's creation of man: "And the LORD God formed man of the dust of the ground, and breathed into his nostrils the breath of life, and man became a living *soul* [my italics]." Actually, that last word in the Hebrew is *nephesh,* and it means a "living being," which is the translation in the New King James Version: "...and man became a living being," and other modern translations.

As I have already stated, the Hebrew Bible does not dwell on an afterlife. Ecclesiastes 9:5 is clear on the subject: "For the living know that they shall die: but the dead know not any thing, neither have they any more a reward...."

There is an air of finality in that verse, just as there is in the following biblical passages: "And Solomon slept with his fathers and was buried in the city of his father David" (1 Kings 11:43). "Omni rested with his ancestors and was buried in Samaria" (1 Kings 16:28). "Ahaz rested with his ancestors and was buried in the city of Jerusalem" (2 Chronicles 28:27).

Ecclesiastes 1:9 concludes with the words:"...there is nothing new under the sun." And what is above the sun, that is, God's realm, is not for us to know. The death of the body marks the end of our being in the world. The Hebrew Bible does not discuss an additional life beyond our world.

What about hell? The Jewish literature of Late Antiquity, especially the Tosefta, a supplement to the Mishnah,[10] contains tales about the Netherworld (She'ol or Gehinnom). Some who wound up in Gehinnom were stuck there forever, while others were condemned for twelve months before their existence was snuffed out. Life in Satan's business establishment was harsh, to say the least. Guests sat in boiling semen or boiling excrement for the duration of their sentence. Ugh! Agony is inadequate to describe their discomfort. (And you thought waterboarding was torture!) Given this scenario, Hitler is in Gehinnom…for eternity. For him, there is no redemption.

If there is a Gehinnom, then Jewish eschatology – and the law of polarity -- also provides for its opposite. The rabbis of old wrote about the world to come (*HaOlam HaBa*), the final reward of the righteous – but provided no details. The usual wording as encountered in the literature is: "All those who belong to Israel [the righteous] have a share in the world to come." And then there are "those who have no portion in the world to come."

Genesis celebrates life – life on planet Earth. It is possible, contrary to statistical probability, that human life may be the only form of intelligent life in the universe. There may be exoplanets (planets orbiting a star outside our solar system) with unicellular life forms, but we may be the only creatures anywhere capable of pondering the mysteries of creation.

Having formed man, God rested on the seventh day and said, "I have done enough; you finish my work." The work of completion for us is *tikkun olam* (from the Hebrew for "repair" + "the world").

---

10   The compilation of the Oral Law into 63 tractates (treatises) by Rabbi Judah ha-Nasi around 200 CE.

There is a *midrash* (rabbinic interpretation and commentary on a biblical passage), *Midrash Rabba, Genesis 11:6*, that states: "All that God created during the six days, He made to be improved." In its functional sense, *tikkun olam* refers to work that improves the world. Whatever we do that makes the world a little better glorifies God.

For those who adhere to the timeline in Genesis, the faith the Jews would develop began with Abraham about 2000 years after his forefather Adam.[11] God made a covenant (*berith* in Hebrew), literally, a contract, with Abraham. "Then he brought him outside and said, 'Look up at the sky and count the stars – if you can count them! Your descendants will be that many!'" (Gen.15:5, CJB[12]).

Well, not quite.[13] We live in a universe whose dimensions are beyond comprehension. The professional star gazers say there are 10 trillion galaxies in the observable universe. Our galaxy, the Milky Way, has 100 billion stars. Thus, the number of stars in the universe is 1 followed by 24 zeros. What's more, astrophysicists discovered that all ordinary, or baryonic, matter accounts for less than 5 percent of the mass of the universe. The rest – over 95 percent – is made up of a mysterious, invisible something-or-another called dark matter and an anti-gravity force called dark energy.

Recently, a group of seven Earth-sized planets orbiting TRAPPIST-1, a dwarf star 40 light years[14] from us, was discovered by NASA astronomers. Three of these rocky exoplanets are in the

---

11   Both Bishop Ussher and the archeologists date Abraham to 2000 B.C., the bishop with certainty, the archeologists, approximately.

12   The Complete Jewish Bible.

13   For the curious, there are, roughly speaking, 7.5×10^{18} power grains of sand in the world.

14   A light-year is the distance light travels in one year. The speed of light has been measured at 186,000 miles per second. Thus, a light-year

habitable zone (where there may be surface liquid water and even life). Other solar systems, and astronomers can now say there are many out there, may also harbor life forms. In other words, we may not be alone in the universe.

Since 1992, the 500th anniversary of Columbus' voyage to the New World, SETI (search for extraterrestrial intelligence) has been listening for radio or optical signals originating from other worlds. We haven't heard from anybody yet and probably won't. That doesn't rule out the possibility intelligent life has existed beyond Earth. As psychiatrist and political commentator Charles Krauthammer has astutely pointed out, intelligent beings may have evolved on faraway planets, only to have destroyed themselves in the end. If life follows a pattern, we humans on Earth, with our own destructive flair, are destined for the same fate.

We *Homo sapiens* are the only humans on earth. Half a dozen species of humans, including *Homo neanderthalensis, Homo erectus,* and *Homo soloensis,* have come and gone.[15] But for the last 10,000 years, the planet has been ours alone. *Homo erectus* was around for 2-million years. How long are we good for?

In what is an awkward segue, I turn to a critical event that occurred in 1991. A black taxi driver named Rodney King was brutally beaten by a quartet of white Los Angeles police officers after a high-speed auto chase, which subsequently set off a series of riots, leaving 55 dead and some 2000 injured. King emerged from the deplorable incident with a memorable quote: "People,

---

is 5.88 trillion miles. Our Milky Way Galaxy is about 150,000 light-years across.

15   According to Michael Shermer, author of *Why Darwin Matters, H. neanderthalensis* should be reclassified as *H. sapiens neanderthalensis,* a subspecies of *H. sapiens.* Shermer would classify *H. erectus* as a separate species on the basis of morphological differences.

I just want to say, can we all get along? Can we get along?" The answer to his question is: No, we can't all get along!

For some, Satan, the monarch of hell, is the answer to why we can't all get along. Then there are those who blame Adam and Eve, who, by sinning against God, saddled our species with a sinful nature. Science has yet to identify a sin gene in the human genome, although, I might add, I don't know if anyone is working on the project. But neuroscience does offer a reasonable explanation for humanity's proclivity to lie, cheat, steal, rage, brutalize others, murder....

In the 1960s, neuroscientist Paul MacLean proposed the idea that the human brain is actually three brains in one. This hypothetical "triune brain" consists of a reptilian core overlaid by a paleomammalian layer and topped by a third layer, the neomammalian, with its highly developed neocortex in humans. For us, life is a tug of war between the older, more primitive parts of our brain and the more recent ratiocinating layering.

I haven't forgotten Adam and Eve, those babes in the woods roboticizing their way around Edenland. This original, guileless pair was no match for polymorphic Satan, who they encountered in their never-never land in serpentine, that is, reptilian form. It was time to leave paradise, and Satan was there to cut the umbilical cord that connected nascent humankind to Mother Earth. Adam and Eve now entered the real world, where their descendants have been walloping and slaying one another ever since – proving to religious fundamentalists that the world belongs to Satan.

We have come far in our development as a species but not far enough to overcome our animal heritage. Many have tried and continue to try to bring out the best in us – to prove we are closer to the angels than to reptilian dinosaurs, those Mesozoic Era creatures that left us an intracranial residue which is part of our brain.

A rabbi living two thousand years ago, Jesus the Galilean Pietist[16] (aka Jesus of Nazareth), defined the good life. He distilled the Ten Commandments of his forefathers down to two statements: love God with everything in you, and love your fellow human beings as yourself. Some have succeeded in guiding their life according to his two precepts – the Catholic Church calls them saints. Many people find it hard just to like their own relatives, let alone try to love seven billion strangers.

Too many of our species are still living at the tooth-and-claw level; they are the ones who are giving *Homo sapiens* a bad reputation and are contributing to what will be humanity's downfall. If I had to summarize what we as a species are in the 21st century, I would say we are a highly developed *mammal* (borrowing language from the late Christopher Hitchens) with all the latent ferocity of the beast. Man's history of repeated genocide is condemnation enough to justify Plautus' assessment of us. Titus Maccius Plautus was a third-century BCE Roman comedic playwright. His most famous play, *Asinaria* ("The Ass-Dealer"), contains a line that has assured Plautus his immortality. There is nothing comical about the line: "*Homo homini lupus est.*" (Man is a wolf to man.)[17]

Since the 1960s, we have been living in the postmodern world – highly secularized, dominated by a population fixated in adolescence, and atavistic. Anything goes as long as it is not traditional. God has been shoved into a corner, for postmoderns understand only too well Dostoevsky's truism from *The Brothers Karamazov*:

16 In Late Antiquity, the Pietists were a small group of maverick preachers who felt so close to Father-God that they addressed him as *Abba* (Daddy). The reader will encounter them in chapter 32.

17 A biblical equivalent to this statement would be Jeremiah 17:9 (KJV): "The heart is deceitful above all things, and desperately wicked: who can know it?" Adequate to describe us as a species, but it could have been worded stronger!

"If there is no God, everything is permitted." For them, the door to a life of self-abandonment is wide open.

Our Zeitgeist calls to mind Judges 17:6: "In those days there was no king [governor, magistrate, or ruler] in Israel, but *every man did that which was right in his own eyes*" (my italics). The Geneva Study Bible comments: "For where there is no Magistrate fearing God, there can be no true religion or order." Disorder characterizes our age – entropy is increasing.

Ever since the dawn of civilization, man has had his gods. The ancient Jews consolidated the gods into one, the LORD God, who stood behind all creation. How this "theo-reform" came about, and Moses' role in the process, is the main, but not only, interest of this volume.

CHAPTER 2

The Bible's applicability and utility are enduring, assuring us that the Adam and Eve narrative is never out of fashion. Change was in the air the day Adam and Eve dared step beyond the borders of their Eden, and change has been the rule of life ever since.

Here in the early 21st century, we find ourselves in a transitional phase concerning the relationship between men and women. The matter runs deep, all the way down to what constitutes men and women. And here there are two views: the biblical and the postmodern feminist.

The biblical view is that there are two sexes: one is called male and the other is called female. You will find this revealing reality in Genesis 5:2: "He [God] created them [us] male and female."

The Bible, the book that made Western civilization possible, is the bane of secular humanists; so to their way of thinking, biblical pronouncements contrary to their point of view have no credence in this the postmodern world. But Genesis 5:2 is scientifically factual, and thus science buttresses the biblical verse.

Again, we, members of the species *Homo sapiens*, have two sexes, and the first words out of the mouth of the delivering obstetrician or midwife are: "It' a boy" or "It's a girl." The determination is made solely by inspection. Sex variations, or intersex (where sexual anatomy doesn't fit the typical definition of male and female) occur about 1 in 1500 to 1 in 2000 births. Therefore, it can be said that the vast majority of people are either male or female, and then there are the errors of nature. Some errors are related to one's protoplasmic integrity, i.e., genetic makeup, and then there are issues of sexuality that originate in the psyche.

The obstetrician, in saying, "It's a boy" or "It's a girl," is designating the baby's sex, not gender. To illustrate the difference between the two terms, let me recall a radio news item heard on the morning of June 18, 2017, concerning pop-culture singer Beyonce, who had given birth to twins: "The genders of the twins have not been disclosed," the announcement concluded. To be correct, the announcer was referring to the babies' *sex*.

Gender is a grammatical term. There are three genders: masculine, feminine, and neuter, e.g., he, she, and it, respectively, as in man, woman, and child. Beyonce's adoring fans wanted to know the sex – male or female, boy or girl – of her twins. Their gender was not what they were asking for.

It takes two people of the opposite sex – not gender – to create a child, and this used to be carried out mainly within the framework of marriage. "What therefore God hath joined together, let not man put asunder" (Mark 10:9), used to be the standard. Marriage in the past was seen as a holy union, and God has always joined a man and a woman in marriage, never two members of the same sex. In our human experience, the union of a man and a woman is a very old institution predating recorded history.

Homosexual marriage has its own history. The most famous of such unions involved the emperor Nero. In 64, he married a freedman, Pythagoras, whom Romans referred to as "one of that filthy herd." The ancient Greeks were tolerant when it came to homosexuality, but Romans looked with contempt on homosexuals. Their Latin term for effeminancy was *Graeculus*, meaning "a little Greek." Homosexuals were considered *unvirtuous*, where the Latin *vir* meant "a real man." Later, Nero married Sporus, a *puer delicates*, a "boy toy," in other words, after first having him castrated. Sporus would play the role of Nero's wife, whereas Pythagoras had functioned as the emperor's husband.

Same-sex marriage was eventually outlawed in the Roman Empire in 342 by Christian emperors Constantius ll and Constans, sons of Constantine the Great. They grew up reading the Bible of their day and were familiar with the passages in Leviticus 18:22; 20:13 and Romans 1:2–27 that condemned homosexuality as an abomination in the eyes of God.

For those who adhere to a Judeo-Christian worldview, the Bible is the ultimate source of truth. Devout Jews and Christians believe in the biblical ethos of their forefathers and live their life accordingly. Thus, viewing homosexuality as anti-God is not equivalent to being homophobic. In fact, Christians are wont to say: Hate the sin, love the sinner.

Today the discussion of sexual deviancy has broadened to include the "in-between" people: transvestites, transgenders, and transsexuals. In our new politicized language, they are "sexual minorities." To be clear, the term deviancy is actually non-judg-mental. Definition-wise, what deviates from the norm is consid-ered deviant. (Nero deviated from the norm to such a degree that he would be labeled perverse.)

When it comes to what constitutes normality, society in this postmodern era has recalibrated its center so as to accommodate all sorts of individuals who do not meet the criteria for what has always been considered normal. To illustrate, at a London teachers conference in 2017, delegates were informed that changing atti-tudes have resulted in a "huge surge in the number of transgender and non-binary people." Are these people abnormal, in the old sense, or merely variants of what society has now come to accept as normal?

Non-binary people? It's time to define some of the terms emanating from the LGBTQ movement. First the more familiar terms. A transvestite is a cross-dresser. The transsexual is someone who identifies as a member of the opposite sex whether or not s/he has undergone a surgical sex change. Transgender applies to any of these and anyone else who does not conform to traditional sexual roles.

"Non-binary people" is the centerpiece in their lexicon. It's synonymous with genderqueer, whose meanings include not being exclusively male or female and shifting between genders – gender floating – depending on one's mood at any given moment. I won't bother to define other queerspeak terms, such as intergender, bi-gender, xenogender, genderfluid, et cetera, although their mean-ings are not all that difficult to fathom.

I see where it's necessary to review some basic facts gleaned from high-school biology. We humans have 23 pairs of chro-mosomes. In women, two of these are Xs; men have an X and a Y, instead of two Xs. That's what defines men and women bio-logically. No matter what kind of hormonal treatment or surgery some people choose in order to change their sexual identity, their biological sex is unaltered.

To summarize, sex indicates male and female and refers to biological differences, which are anatomical and physiological. Gender, in its non-grammatical usage, refers to the role of (some) males and females in society (gender role), or a person's sexual self-identity (gender identity). Transgender people have a sense of personal identity and gender identity that does not match up with their birth identity. From Mario Puzo's *The Godfather*, Luca Brazi says to Don Corleone on the wedding of his daughter, "May their first child be a masculine child." Brasi, of course, meant a boy, one who would grow up, and now in 2018 we have to interject, with a full complement of masculine traits.

Back to life across the Sea of Atlas, Britain's largest labor union, the National Union of Teachers, NUT for short, is out to teach children as young as 2 years about the transgender life and same-sex relationships. No, I didn't come up with this foolishness while in a delirium, and it isn't fake news. A number of reporters covered NUT's annual conference over the Easter 2017 weekend in Cardiff, Wales.

The general secretary of the NUT added, "This is the 21st century...It's high time that PSHE [Personal, Social and Health Education] and SRE [Sex and Relationship Education] – including LGBT+ education – is recognized as an essential part of the school curriculum." The quote is from an article, "Teach toddlers about transgender issues, NUT says," by the education editor of *The Daily Telegraph*, London (April 17, 2017). Grimms' fairy tales yield to Rod Serling's *Twilight Zone*!

If there is a takeaway, it would be: sex is a matter of the body while gender exists in the mind.

Some readers of these words may remember the Billy Wilder farce *Some Like It Hot* starring Jack Lemmon and Tony Curtis.

They play a pair of prohibition Era musicians who witness a mob murder in Chicago (where else!) and fearful for their lives, find refuge in an all-girl band – disguised in high heels, swanky dresses, and dripping with makeup. No one in 1959, when the film was released, saw sexual pathology in what the two main characters were doing on screen. It was all innocent movie-land fun. However, the age of innocence was about to run its course as we entered the Sixties. The modern world ended, and the postmodern era came rushing in like a tsunami.

In the postmodern world, here in what has become Alice in AmericaLand, unreason has replaced reason and unreality has replaced reality. The secular humanists now not only run society, but they also shape the culture. Ever since the Sixties, the fanatical feminist wing of the National Organization for Women, the feminatics, has been inching us toward an androgynous society.

There are two sexes but three (grammatical) genders. They favor the third of these, the neuter gender. Reduce the male to an androgyne, a neuter, and they will have won the battle of the sexes. Just survey the college scene for an insight into what is going on today: droves of young snowflakes, among their other developmental issues, are in distress (dysphoric in the new vocabulary) over or not sure of their expected male or female roles. For them, manhood and womanhood are alien concepts – they have been raised to think of themselves in terms of personhood, which is a *neutered* state.

In a nutshell, the feminatics, along with their witting and unwitting allies, harbor a fear or *hatred of* masculinity, technically referred to as andrismophobia (from Gk *andrismos*, masculinity). It is psychopathology of the first order.

The most nettlesome of the feminatics are in the hallowed halls of ivy. In the realm of these oxytocin-deficient, castrating dragonettes, transgender ideology trumps the realities of biology.

Nowhere is that better illustrated than in Michael Rectenwald's *Springtime for Snowflakes* (2018). Rectenwald, a professor of Liberal Studies at New York University, was on the receiving end of a verbal exchange with an uber-feminist colleague, who "seemed to mockingly suggest that I must believe *retrograde gender ideas like the reality of sex difference*" (my italics). For those of us who function in the world of reality, sex differences are most definitely real. And reality, for those who need it defined, is the way things actually are, not the way you fancy them to be.

The Christian Bible furnishes us a *diagnosis* for these outlandish academics: "And for this cause, God shall send them strong delusion, that they should believe a lie" (2 Corinthians 2:11).

In delusional disorders, a person holds fast to a false belief in the face of proof to the contrary. The listing in the latest *Diagnostic and Statistical Manual of Mental Disorders*, 5th Edition, for an individual displaying the "feminaticism" alluded to above would be Delusional Disorder, unspecified type, 297.1.

Mother Nature is not on the side of democracy. Her concern is the survival of our species, not the individual. Our democratically oriented society considers every life to be precious (except the preborn) and will enact laws to protect those deemed vulnerable. Males with Klinefelter syndrome,[18] for example, are sterile and thus dispensable, as far as Nature is concerned. What matters to her is that we continue to reproduce ourselves in sufficient numbers to keep our species viable. How we do that in terms of our human dramas doesn't move her in the least. For certainty, androgyny, the direction in which we are drifting, or more accurately, being led, is a dead end for the human species.

---

18   Born with cells that have an extra X chromosome and are 47,XXY instead of 46,XY.

Nature – and I interpret nature to be an agency of God – prefers to hear us sing out: *Vive la difference.* What the feminatics refer to as equality equates to sameness, the opposite of how nature works: she prefers differences. If you want equality, be an amoeba. Amoebae reproduce by binary fission, that is, by splitting into two equal daughter cells. They're all the same. God's plan for us would never have gotten very far if that's all He had in mind for life on Mother Earth.

If they were with us today, would Eve join the women's empowerment movement, and would Adam choose virility over proto-androgyny? For Eve, we can say: Baby, you've come a long way. For Adam, well, he's no longer ruler of the roost. Realistically, the biblical Adam and Eve wouldn't last a day in today's world!

As already pointed out, our world changed drastically in the 1960s when we went from the modern to the postmodern age. It was a traumatic – I might even say cataclysmic – time in history.

We reserve the term Cultural Revolution for the young people's militant uprising that occurred in China under Mao Tse-tung during the 1960s. Our cultural revolution had a name of sorts: it was clled the Counterculture. Usually, it was not capitalized, but its importance is such that the term deserves to begin in upper case. It marked the beginning of the postmodern world.

History is replete with events that have "changed the world," an expression repeated so often it begins to sound like a cliché. But the Counterculture will be viewed by future historians as a turning point in human history.

How did it all begin? Well, my own first awareness of the changing cultural scene came in September 1963, when I was a third-year medical student at McGill University in Montreal. I had been living and studying in Europe for a number of years, and what was going on in North America caught me by surprise when I returned home to Maine.

During my rotation in psychiatry, I saw a distressed young woman who, in between copious tears, managed to convey the reason for her distress. She thrust a copy of Betty Friedan's *The Feminine Mystique* (1963) into my hands and proceeded to explain Friedan's new feminist vision of womankind, which was in marked contrast to the biblical world view that had shaped her own upbringing.

Of course, Betty Friedan wasn't the first crusading feminist to appear on the horizon, but her book was the catalyst that fueled the post-World War ll movement. Historically, French feminist philosopher Simone Beauvoir's *The Second Sex* preceded *The Feminine Mystique*. Published in 1949, *The Second Sex* may be said to have touched off second-wave feminism, the movement that began in the early '60s. Second-wave feminism expanded first-wave feminism (time frame the 19th and early 20th century), which was concerned with voting rights and property rights, to include reproductive rights, inequalities in the work place, domestic violence, et cetera. As for the content of *The Second Sex*, de Beauvoir saw history as the story of women's oppression: "humanity is male, and man defines woman."

How far back do we want to go to pinpoint the origins of feminism? Mary Wollstonecraft, mother of *Frankenstein* novelist Mary Shelley, wrote an early feminine treatise, *A Vindication of the Rights of Women* (1792). Wollstonecraft argued that women were good for more than the 3 K's: *Kinder, Kuche, Kirche* (children, cooking, church). She believed the distaff side was ready for *cognitionis*, Latin for "knowledge."

We can go back to antiquity to identify women of exceptional talent who could be considered "proto-feminists," such as the Greek poetess Sappho, from the island of Lesbos (better known for her lesbianism than her poetry); Hypatia of Alexandria, a pagan scholar who taught philosophy and mathematics at the university; and Eleanor of Aquitaine, who parleyed her mastery of the art of mixing sex and politics to become one of the most dominant figures of 12th-century Europe.

From my late wife, Chen-Wu, I learned about the first-century Pan Chao, the preeminent woman scholar of China: historian, astronomer, mathematician, poetess, essayist, and national librarian. Empress Deng Sui called her the "Gifted One." Pan Chao wrote *Lessons for Women*, a Confucian guide for women's conduct. The book, I should point out, stressed family harmony.

Since the name of Confucius has come up, I should say something about yin and yang theory. Confucianism underscores yang's dominant, male characteristics (while Taoism, on the other hand, accentuates yin's subordinate, female features). In Pan Chao, despite her Confucian orientation, yin and yang were not in conflict but in harmony, which may help explain her enormous intellectual productivity and the ease with which she maneuvered through her patriarchal society. In psychological terms, not "conflicted" for Pan Chao meant she was free from emotional confusion and distress caused by opposing psychological forces.

At court, she rocked the cradle of the infant Emperor Shang of Han. I think she would have appreciated 19th-century William Ross Wallace's poem "The Hand That Rocks the Cradle Is the Hand That Rules the World," a paean to motherhood, the *vis a tergo* that helps drive humanity forward.

In summary, what the radical feminists -- now allied with a recently developed LGBTQ movement -- fantasize is a unisex realm, where male power has been neutralized. God's design, beginning with Adam and Eve, calls for two sexes to accomplish His plan. And what is His plan? To try to fathom His plan, you have to start with basics, and so you *begin the journey* with Leviticus 19:2: "You shall be holy, for I the LORD your God am holy." To get started begin by reviewing the Ten Commandments and then study Leviticus 19....

CHAPTER 3

M ost readers of the Hebrew Bible in English aren't aware that more than a third of its contents is poetry, but the poetry isn't like what they read in school. We in the western world think in a stepwise, logical fashion, where one event or idea follows another. The approach of the Hebrew writers living in the ancient East was to group similar ideas together. Another distinction, our English poetry is essentially sound-based, whereas biblical poetry is thought-based. It contains quite a bit of what is called parallelism, which I will explain with examples. Hebrew parallelism can become rather complicated; so I will confine myself to the simpler forms.

Structurally, the simplest form of parallelism is synonymous parallelism, where two lines express the same thought in different words. An example is Isaiah 59:9: "Therefore, judgment is far from us:/And righteousness does not reach us." In biblical Hebrew (and New Testament Greek), justice and righteousness mean the same thing.

You encounter synonymous parallelism in Job 33:4: "The spirit of God hath made me, and the breath of the Almighty hath given me life." Here the second clause repeats the opening clause but with different wording. God's breath in Hebrew is *ruach*, which also means spirit, mind, and wind.[19]

You can miss parallelism if you read too fast. For instance, it would be easy to overlook it in Genesis 15:17: "And it came to pass, that, when the sun went down, and it was dark...." When the sun goes down, it's dark; and when it's dark, the sun has gone down.

In antithetic parallelism, couplets (or triplets) express contrasting thoughts, as in Psalm 1:6: "For the LORD watches over the way of the righteous,/But the way of the wicked will perish."

In synthetic parallelism, the second part adds something new to the first part or explains it. You find this in Psalm 14:2, for example: "The LORD looked down from heaven upon the children of men,/to see if there were any that did understand, and seek God."

All the prophets' writings, with the exception of Haggai and Malachi, contain poetry. Habakkuk, who prophesied in the 7th-century BCE, made extensive use of chiasmus, sometimes referred to as inverted parallelism, where elements of a sentence are repeated but in reverse order. Shakespeare's three witches open *Macbeth* with a chiasmus: "Fair is foul, and foul is fair." Jesus liked to use chiastic structures. In Mark 2:27, he says: "The Sabbath was made for man, not man for the Sabbath," [Sabbath-man-man-Sabbath

---

19 In 1 Kings 19:11, where Elijah meets God at Horeb: "...And, behold, the LORD passed by, and a great and strong wind rent the mountains, and brake in pieces the rocks before the LORD, but the LORD was not in the wind..." Here we have what can be called a false allusion to God being in the wind, for in this case, He turns out to be "a still small voice." It's definite in Acts 2:2, when on the day of Pentecost, "...suddenly there came a sound from heaven as of a rushing mighty wind, and it filled all the house where they were sitting." God's *ruach* was present and filled the apostles.

– a-b-b-a construction] and in Matthew 20:16, "So the last shall be first, and the first last." John Kennedy resorted to chiasmus in his inaugural address in January 1961: "Ask not what your country can do for you – ask what you can do for your country."[20]

Habakkuk employed chiasmus, gender-matched parallelism, staircase parallelism, climactic parallelism, and pivot-pattern parallelism, along with changes in word order and the use of tricola (plural of tricolon – sentences made up of three parts of equal length).

A tricolon consisting of only three successive words is a hendiatris, and nearly everyone is familiar with at least one such tricolon. Following his quick victory over Pharnace, king of Bosphorus, in 47 BCE, Julius Caesar wrote the Senate: *Veni, vidi, vici* ("I came, I saw, I conquered.")

A fitting hendiatris to describe today's secularized America would be: power, money, sex, the new telluric trinity of half the population. Immorality, infidelity, incivility would be another appropriate hendiatris.

Back to the prophet. Habakkuk is the consummate poet, and his rich poetry also included simile and metaphor, allegory, metonymy, merismus (figure of speech in which the whole thought is implied by naming two of its parts),[21] hendiadys (expressing one idea using two words connected by "and"),[22] hyperbole, paronomasia (a play on words), personification, synecdoche (a literary device in which a part of something represents the whole, or vice versa;

---

20 A mother of 5 adolescents posted a sign on her refrigerator door: "Ask not what your mother can do for you; ask what you can do for your mother."

21 As an example, "God created the heavens and the earth (Genesis 1:1). The thought is: God created the universe.

22 Example, "...they rejoice and are glad" (Habakkuk 1:15). To rejoice is to experience joy and gladness to a high degree.

an example would be: all hands on deck), alliteration, assonance, enjambment (a sentence or thought that does not end with the line but continues to the next line),[23] et cetera. And you thought he was just a *minor* prophet – and if dropped from that list of twelve, he wouldn't be missed!

CHAPTER 4

A few words about the organization of the Hebrew Bible is in order. It is customary to divide the Holy Book into three sections: Torah ("Teaching"), Nevi'im ("Prophets"), and Ketuvim (Writings"), yielding an acronym, Tanakh. The first section of the Tanakh, the Torah, also referred to as Five Books of Moses and the Pentateuch (Gk. *penta*, five + *teukhos*, book, scroll), consists of five books: Genesis, Exodus, Leviticus, Numbers, and Deuteronomy. In Deuteronomy 34:5, Moses dies after God shows him the Promised Land from Mount Nebo, and Joshua then begins the conquest of Canaan. Some scholars extend the Pentateuch to include the Book of Joshua, which begins where Deuteronomy ends, thus creating the portmanteau Hexateuch. For that matter, there is even a Heptateuch, the Pentateuch plus Joshua and Judges. Moses' inclusion here is understandable since he wears several hats in Exodus, including that of judge – he is the

---

23 From Keats' "Endymion": "A thing of beauty is a thing forever:/Its loveliness increases, it will never/Pass into nothingness but still will keep/A bower quiet for us, and sleep/Full of sweet dreams...."

first of the Judges. So of these seven books, my particular favorite is Exodus.

On the one hand, Exodus is part of sacred Scripture, which is the way worshippers approach it. Then again, Exodus is also literature, epic literature; that is, Exodus is the epic story of the Jewish people. The story developed first, and the liturgical dimension was added later as Judaism itself gradually developed.

As epic literature, the Book of Exodus belongs on the same shelf in public and university libraries with the world's epic tales: the Ugaritic epic poem *Legend of Keret*; Homer's *Iliad* and *Odyssey*; Virgil's *Aeneid*; Dante's *Divine Comedy*; Spain's *The Poem of the Cid*; the Hindu's *Mahabharata*; France's national epic, *The Song of Roland*; the Old English epic poem *Beowulf*, et cetera. Each epic has its hero: Moses in Exodus, King Keret of Khuburu in the Ugaritic epic poem, Achilles in the *Iliad*, Beowulf in *Beowulf*, Karna in the *Mahabharata*, and so forth.

Moses is the subject of our concern. His story is familiar to children of all three Abrahamic religions: Judaism, Christianity, and Islam. For countless generations, the biblical account had been accepted as factual, but questions as to its historical accuracy began to surface as early as the 17th century and developed into a movement referred to as "historical criticism" and also "higher criticism." Today many people, including numerous if not most scholars in the field, consider the biblical story of Moses more legend than historical fact.

Biblical scholar and archeologist Philip Davies, for instance, wrote, "Moses himself has about as much historic reality as King Arthur." Historian Tom Holland commented, "The likelihood that the biblical story records an actual event is fairly small." What mythologist Samuel Henry Hooke had to say in his *Middle Eastern Mythology* about King Keret, "Some substratum of historical tradition may underlie this curious legend," could hold true for Moses and the Exodus as well. Archeologist William Dever writes with surgical precision: "The whole 'Exodus-Conquest' cycle of stories must now be set aside as largely mythical... tales told primarily to validate religious beliefs."

Does it really matter if Moses didn't do all the things the biblical account ascribes to him? Is he to be consigned to that make-believe realm where we find Hercules, King Arthur, and Robin Hood? For Asher Ginzberg (1856–1927), who wrote under his Hebrew name Ahad Ha-'Am, it doesn't matter. In his critically important 1904 essay, "Moses,"[24] he explained that Moses is Moses regardless of what the critics think.

What Asher Ginzberg says in "Moses" can be distilled down into one sentence: *The Moses that matters is the Moses of memory.* Audiences are surprised when they hear me utter that last word. They are expecting me to end the sentence with "history." Ginzberg started something new, a fresh approach to understanding Moses and the Exodus.

That was Ginzberg writing in 1904. Now let's fast forward to the end of the century, to the German Egyptologist Jan Assmann, whom I dub the dean of contemporary Egyptologists. His first book, which I read when it came out in 1998, is entitled *Moses the Egyptian: The Memory of Egypt in Western Monotheism.* I won't say anything about the book here – or about the other nine he has authored to date on ancient Egypt – because the title itself suggests a different avenue of exploration into the Moses story than the biblical account I am following. However, I will deal with Assmann's approach later.

Nevertheless, Assmann's essential thinking can be boiled down to one sentence, which is actually quoting him: "*The way history is remembered is more important than the way it really was.*" Assmann's

---

24   From *Selected Essays of Ahad Ha-'Am*, translated by Leon Simon, 1912.

antithetically worded statement may leave you baffled. You don't want memories. You want facts – Moses' history as it really was.

Here's the reality. Moses belongs somewhere in the second millennium BCE.[25] As such, he is beyond the reach of the historian. The historian must wait for the archeologist to dig something up before he can write something. Moses exists in the long ago, in the time of memories, not in historical time. With Moses, we are not dealing with history per se but with mnemohistory, history based on memory, not historical fact. The term, coined by Assmann, comes from mnemonics, the study of memory. (The word derives from Mnemosyne, goddess of memory in Greek mythology.)

CHAPTER 5

The Hebrew epic begins with a three-month-old infant, the son of Levite parents and the future hero of his people, bundled up in a watertight basket amidst the Nile bank's reeds and rushes, hidden there by a distraught mother. Pharaoh[26] had issued a decree that all male Hebrew newborns were to be drowned, and his guards were making an unannounced sweep of the Hebrew quarter. They were accompanied by several Egyptian mothers with nurslings of their own forced to cry so that even carefully

---

25   BCE (Before the Common Era) and CE (Common Era) are coming into usage in the non-Christian world, supplementing B.C. and A.D., respectively.

26   Egyptian term for "king." The pharaoh mentioned here would be Seti I.

sequestered Hebrew infants would then start crying – referred to by psychologists as emotional contagion – and give themselves away. Once the search was over, the baby's mother would retrieve him from his hiding place in the Nile. Then again, the biblical account leaves the reader with an alternate interpretation: the infant could have been positioned in a spot along the river so as to be found.

Fate, destiny, Providence, God, or whatever other equivalent term one may come up with, does intervene. The baby is rescued from the river by a princess identified as Pharaoh's daughter. Observing the scene is the infant's (seven-year-old) sister, not at all shy in the presence of royalty, who, calmly, volunteers her mother as a wet nurse for her baby brother.

The Moses birth story has parallels in other cultures. For instance, Sargon's birth and early life are described in a 7th-century B.C. Neo-Assyrian text: "My high priestess mother conceived me, in secret she bore me. She set me in a basket of rushes, with bitumen she sealed my lid. She cast me into the river...The river bore me up and carried me to Akki, the drawer of water. Akki... took me as his son and reared me." Akki was a royal gardener in the Sumerian city of Kish (founded ca. 3100 BCE) – and the step-father of Sargon the Great (reigned ca. 2340–2284 BCE), founder of the Akkadian Empire and one of the earliest of the world's great empire builders.

In Roman mythology, the newborn twins Romulus and Remus are condemned to death by King Amulius, but the servant ordered to carry out the sentence takes pity on the infants and places them in a basket. They float down the Tiber River to a cave where they are suckled by a she-wolf and eventually are rescued by the shepherd Faustulus and his wife Acca Larentia. Romulus grows up to become the first king of Rome, which he founded in 753 BCE.

In the Hindu epic, the *Mahabharata* [from Sanskrit *maha*, great + *bharata*, story], the unwed princess Kunti beseeches the sun god Surya to grant her a son, and he answers her prayer: "Thus, by the grace of Lord Surya, Kunti conceived." (Cf. the Holy Spirit and Mary in the Jesus birth narrative.) She places her illegitimate infant in a basket and floats him down the Ashva river. He is rescued by Adhiratha, a charioteer of King Dhritarashtra of Hastinapur, and he and his wife Radha raise the child as their own. As Karna, he goes on to become the tragic hero of the Kurukshetra war.[27]

I'll interrupt the flow for a moment to explain that Karna means "ear" in Sanskrit. Kunti gave birth to him through her ear. Such unconventional births are encountered from time to time in the ancient literature. In Greek mythology, the goddess Athena sprang from the forehead of Zeus, an illustration of the male giving birth to the female. Uranus, ruler of the Titans, was castrated by his son Cronus, and Aphrodite (Gk. *aphros* means "foam"), Uranus' daughter, was born from the white foam given off from her father's castrated genitals. In the Hebrew Bible, in one version, God created Eve by fashioning her from one of Adam's ribs.

From the time of Stone Age cultures down to the early 2nd millennium BCE, men stood in awe at woman's ability to bring forth life. Thus, the dominance of the goddesses, including Gaia (Mother Earth) providing us with the "offspring," that is, produce of the earth. But by the middle of the 2nd millennium BCE, we saw the rise of male power. The Babylonian god Marduk defeated the primordial goddess Tiamat in battle, symbolic of a new world ordering that would be patriarchal.

---

27 Also called the Mahabharata War. Tradition dates it to 3102 BCE, but "the historicity of the war remains subject to scholarly discussions," quoting archeologist and academic Timothy Insoll.

In another account, Acrisius, king of Argos, sealed his daughter Danae and her infant son Perseus in a chest and set them adrift at sea, because an oracle had warned him that he would be killed by a son born to Danae. Zeus' brother, Poseidon, guided the chest to the island of Seriphos, where the fisherman Dictys (name means "Mr. Net") found them. (One characteristic of the legendary hero was his ability to survive an attempt on his life when an infant, usually by a father fearing his throne would be usurped by an offspring.)

In the biblical account, the hero as a baby does not float down the Nile in his basket, which has been reinforced with pitch as in the Sargon birth account, because he would then wind up in the Mediterranean. All these babies-in-the-river tales have certain similarities, and the fact that they diverge in detail does not negate the idea that they spring from a common source deep within the mind of man, as explained in the following paragraph.

To these four illustrations can be added stories about other mythologized heroes, tales that contain a corresponding identifying strand, referred to as a mytheme. Psychoanalyst Otto Rank, one of Freud's inner circle, zeroed in on the shared essence, the mytheme, found in the stories about Oedipus, Paris, Telephus, Gilgamesh, Cyrus the Great, Tristan, and others in *The Myth of the Birth of the Hero* (1912). In Jungian psychology, there are mythic characters and elements found in the collective unconscious of people the world over, which he labeled archetypes. Of the various Jungian archetypes, here we are dealing with *the hero*.

Returning to chapter 2 of Exodus, we have already been introduced to a handful of major characters in the Moses story: the infant, his parents and sister, and a princess identified as Pharaoh's daughter. All five characters have one thing in common: not one of them is named. The first to be named will be the infant (q.v.).

His sister has proposed a Hebrew wet nurse, none other than the baby's, and her own, mother whom the princess readily accepts: "Take this child away, and nurse it for me..." (Ex. 2:9, KJV). The passage continues: "and I will give thee thy wages."

Actually, what is in the text about the infant is covered in 8 short verses – Exodus 2:2–9. What you read in these passages falls into the category of storytelling, not historical fact. Biblical inerrancy advocates may judge such a statement to be heretical, but as I have already pointed out, my approach to an analysis of the Book of Exodus is from a literary perspective. As stated earlier, *first came the literature*, the storytelling, most of it orally transmitted with some of it written, and subsequently its incorporation into the liturgy as it was being developed.

Historically, wet-nursing in ancient Egypt was a lively industry with established procedures. Wet nurses were hired on a contractual basis, anywhere from three months to three years, with obligations of both parties clearly written out. A physician would determine the quality of the wet-nurse's milk: breast milk that smelled like fish disqualified the candidate.[28] She could not become pregnant for the duration of the contract, for that would affect lactation. We also have to remember that Egypt in the time of the Exodus was a "phallo-dominant," that is, patriarchal society; so breast-feeding contracts were negotiated by the wet nurse's husband. The text doesn't mention the nursling's father, Amram, in this connection. The princess, despite her royal status, may not have been able to participate in the negotiations, which would have been handled by a male aide.

---

28   A popular home remedy to increase the flow of milk was to stew the dorsal fin of a Nile perch in oil and rub the oil on the mother's back. We weren't taught that in obstetrics/gynecology in medical school!

In the Exodus account, the baby's Hebrew mother, Yochebed, became his wet nurse: her official designation would be "royal wet nurse." Royal wet nurses were held in high esteem at court. Teye, for example, was the wet nurse of Nefertiti, Akhenaten's queen. She and her husband, Ay, went on to hold influential positions in the king's palace, with Ay eventually even becoming pharaoh. Yochebed, as a royal wet nurse, would have joined the princess' household at court, but there is no indication in the Exodus text that she did so; and the presumption is she continued to breast feed her infant son while living in Goshen until she surrendered the child to the princess at age three.

Archeological and biblical sources seem to agree that children were weaned by the age of three years in both ancient Egypt and also Israel. In the *Instruction of Ani*, an Egyptian wisdom text, the scribe Ani working in the court of Nefertari, principal wife of Ramesses ii, reminds his son, "When your time was due and you were born, she [your mother] accepted the burden of *having* her breast in your mouth for three years."

In 2 Maccabees 7:27, the mother of seven sons being tortured to death by Antiochus for refusing to eat swine's flesh, exhorts her youngest son to be brave: "O my son, have pity on me that bore thee nine months in my womb, and suckled thee three years."

There is still the question raised above of the princess paying wages to a Hebrew slave. Would Yochebed be paid the going rate or a lower rate because of her social status? The question leads to another question. We have been taught that there were twelve tribes in bondage. But were there? Actually, the Levites, the priestly tribe, were not in bondage. The Egyptians had great respect for those who were dedicated to their god in an official capacity. All the Hebrew priests were Levites, although not all Levites were priests; however, in one way or another, they all did serve their god El Shaddai – some attended to the priests, others functioned as teachers of their god, et cetera.

If they were not in bondage – and this is the second question – why were their newborn being put to death? They should have been immune to Pharaoh' edict, you would think, but they apparently were not. Another historical mystery, it seems. Then again, Exodus is not a historical document. It's a story purporting to relate historical facts; but it is mnemohistory, based more on memory than what we today consider fact. Another way to word it, the Exodus text contains memories that echo down to us from the 13th century BCE, the time most scholars in the field place Moses and the Exodus.

One thing the reader becomes aware of early on in the Book of Exodus is the meager amount of information furnished by the author, opening the door for scholars and others to expand upon the material presented. Also there are extra-biblical sources of more than passing interest available to us, such as the writings of the 3rd-century BCE Egyptian priest and historian Manetho and the Greek geographer and historian Strabo (64 BCE-24 CE). In *Aegyptiaca*, Manetho described Moses as an Egyptian, not a Hebrew, who lived during the reign of Amenhotep lll and his son Amenhotep lV/Akhenaten. He does mention an Israelite exodus that occurred under a later pharaoh, Ramses (also spelled Ramesses, Rameses, and Ramose).

Strabo wrote about Moses in his *Geography*: "...the Egyptians were the ancestors of the present Jews. An Egyptian priest named Moses, who possessed a portion of the country called Lower Egypt...being dissatisfied with the established institutions there, left it and came to Judaea with a large body of people who worshipped the Divinity...."

Early Christian writers did much the same thing. We have the birth narrative concerning Jesus of Nazareth, but after that we know preciously little of his early life until the age of 12, when we find the future rabbi dialoguing with the elders (Pharisees) in the Jerusalem temple (Luke 2:39–52). Jesus disappears from view again until he is about 30, when he enters upon the world stage to begin his ministry.

Several dozen non-canonical gospels attempt to fill in the gaps. The Infancy Gospel of Thomas describes Jesus' life as a child and is filled with events of a supernatural nature, e.g., Jesus, at age five, fashioning a dozen sparrows out of clay that he then brings to life and healing his brother James who is bitten by a poisonous snake. In the Infancy Gospel of James, Joseph is described as a widower with children. The Gospel of Peter, which focuses on the passion narrative, ascribes responsibility for the Crucifixion to Herod Antipas, not Pontius Pilate. In 367 CE, Athanasius, Bishop of Alexandria, narrowed down the multitude of writings on Jesus in circulation to 27 books (eventually the official canon); these included only four Gospels – Mark, Matthew, Luke and John.

Returning to Moses and the Exodus after this brief detour into the New Testament, two questions audiences usually want to have answered are: Where and when in Egypt is our story taking place? The early setting, in chapter 2, is the eastern Nile Delta in Lower Egypt near the Mediterranean Sea. The Nile originates in central Africa and flows north. The southern part of Egypt is called Upper Egypt and the rest is Lower Egypt, which includes the Nile Delta.

In the 13th century BCE, the time of Moses and the Exodus, the Nile divided into seven branches, or distributaries, in the Delta before flowing into the Mediterranean. We're interested in the two easternmost branches, the Tanitic and to its east the Pelusiac. Between the two was Goshen, located on the western bank of the Pelusiac, which was where the 12 Hebrew tribes were housed.

For most of pharaonic Egypt's history, Lower Egypt was divided into 20 nomes, or districts, and Upper Egypt into 22 nomes. Goshen, in Lower Egypt, was nome 20, choice land with soil and grass ideal for farming and raising livestock. Nome 20 was the easternmost district of Egypt and represented the country's frontier. The pharaohs were happy and relieved to have the descendants of Joseph, whose ancestors were a fierce warrior people, guarding the border for them.

The time is more difficult to ascertain. There are two major timelines: one is the scholars'; the other is biblical. For the scholars, the consensus is that the Exodus occurred during the middle of the 13th century BCE, somewhere around 1250 BCE, which, if nothing else, is an easy number to remember.

Following the text, Moses was 80 years old at the time of the Exodus, which means he was born in 1330 (1250 + 80 = 1330). The author divides Moses' life into three equal parts: 40 years in Egypt, 40 years in Midian, and 40 years wandering around in the desert.[29] He died at the age of 120 in what would have been 1210 BCE. For the curious, his former nemesis, Pharaoh Ramesses II, died in 1213. Of note, the Merenptah Stele, created c.1208, includes the earliest recorded mention of Israel. The dates cited in the previous two sentences are considered to be fairly accurate. However, history does not record with such surety the exact year of Moses' death nor his age.

Merenptah ruled Egypt after his father, Rameses II, from 1213 to 1204 BCE. "Israel is laid waste, its seed is not" (also translated as "Israel is wasted, bare of seed"), is the only mention of Israel in ancient Egyptian records. Is the statement itself true, and does the inscription actually mention Israel? The stele, a black granite slab ten feet in height, was discovered by the preeminent English Egyptologist Sir Flinders Petrie in 1896 at Thebes. It is also known as the "Israel Stele," because a *majority* [my italics] of

29   And the Book of Exodus is divided into 40 chapter.

scholars translate one hieroglyph in the inscription as "Israel" – but then, and this should not be overlooked or dismissed, there are alternative translations of the glyph.

The stele describes Merenptah's victory over the Libu, an ancient Berber tribe from which the name Libya is derived, Meshwesh Libyans and the Sea Peoples (the Philistines of the Bible). Near the bottom of the stele, the king refers to an earlier military campaign in Canaan, where he defeated Ashkelon, Gezer, Yanoam, and Israel. The distinguished German philologist Wilhelm Spiegelberg[30] was hired by Flinders Petrie to translate the stele, but he was puzzled by one hieroglyph. Petrie, in a moment of inspiration – and don't forget, Spiegelberg, not Petrie, is the language maven here – blurted out: "Israel," and the noted philologist acquiesced. Translating inscriptions accurately is difficult, to be sure, but at times what the experts come up with is *subjective interpretation.*[31]

Ashkelon, Gezer, and Yanoam were established cities, while "Israel" seemed to refer to a semi-nomadic or a marginally settled crop-growing people dwelling in the highlands of Canaan. The expression "wasted, bare of seed" was standard language at the time to indicate victory over an enemy with destruction of their grain supply. This would lead to famine the following year, thus neutralizing them as a military threat. Destroying an enemy's "seed" could also mean killing their fighting force of young men, leaving no one or few men to continue to produce offspring.

In 2012, I came across an article about a trio of Egyptologists/ biblical scholars, Manfred Gorg, Peter van der Veen, and

---

30 Spiegelberg accompanied the novelist Thomas Mann to Egypt, helping draft his *Joseph and His Brothers* tetralogy.

31 Quoting Samuel Butler, "Life is the art of drawing sufficient conclusions from insufficient premises." But not in philology!

Christoffer Theis, who placed "Israel" in Egypt even earlier than the late 13th century BCE. They examined a broken statue pedestal containing hieroglyphs housed in the Egyptian Museum of Berlin and *suggested* [my italics] that one of the hieroglyphs designated "Israel." The inscription is dated to around 1400 BCE, which is some 200 years earlier than the Merenptah Stele. Predictably, not all scholars agree with the Gorg-van der Veen-Theis interpretation of the inscription.[32]

Douglas Petrovich, archeologist, epigrapher,[33] and professor of ancient Egyptian studies at Wilfrid Laurier University in Waterloo, Canada, published *The World's Oldest Alphabet: Hebrew as the Language of the Proto-Consonantal Script* in 2016, which immediately sparked controversy in the Egyptology community. If his work holds up, it will be as important to biblical studies as Darwin's *On the Origin of Species by Means of Natural Selection* has been to biology. Petrovich is telling us that it was the ancient Hebrews who, in the 19th century BCE, turned 22 hieroglyphs into letters and thus created the first alphabet, preceding the Phoenicians, long credited for developing the earliest alphabet around 1050 BCE.

What is the non-expert to make of Petrovich's proposal that the earliest alphabetic inscriptions are Hebrew? In his introduction to the book, Eugene Merrill, Distinguished Professor of Old Testament Studies (Emeritus) at Dallas Theological Seminary, wrote that Petrovich's "expertise in epigraphy, paleography, lexicography, and comparative linguistics and literature has led him to the conviction that of all options one can currently advance as to the ultimate origins of the alphabet, the identification of proto-Hebrew is the very best candidate...."

32 Simply stated, Egyptology is not hard science.
33 Epigraphy is the study of inscriptions.

Pastor Jimmy R. Reagan, writing in his blog, "The Reagan Review," proclaims *The World's Oldest Language* to be a "boon... to those of us who believe in the complete veracity of the Bible."

Aren M. Wilson-Wright, of the University of Zurich, writes: "[It] is unclear that Hebrew existed as a distinct language during the Middle Kingdom [2055 BCE-1650 BCE], when many of the early alphabetic inscriptions were written."

In his critique of *The World's Oldest Alphabet*, heavyweight scholar Dr. Thomas Schneider, Professor of Egyptology, University of British Columbia, commented that Petrovich's interpretation of the inscriptions he studied "will not get traction with scholars who work in...Palaeography and Comparative Semitics."

The most biting commentary I came across was written by a young scholar who identified himself only as Nathaniel: "The book is nothing more than an exercise in Christian apologetics, written to defend the idea of an historical exodus."

Dr. Christopher A. Rollston, of the Department of Classical and Near Eastern Languages and Civilizations, George Washington University, wrote: "In short, the things that Douglas Petrovich considers to be markers of Hebrew are, in fact, just markers of the Semitic languages in general...Thus, the Early Alphabetic inscriptions from Serabit el-Khadem and Wadi el-Hol are definitely not Hebrew."

The inscription from Serabit el-Khadem in the Sinai Peninsula, written in an early Semitic script, is dated to about 1500 BCE, and the Wadi el-Hol inscription found in Egypt, also written in an early Semitic script, is about 4000 years old.

I find myself caught between two currents. As a non-expert, I will just have to wait and see what happens. In the meantime, I accept the consensus thinking that the Hebrew script developed from the Phoenician script around 1000 BCE.

Besides the 13th-century date, there is an alternate dating for the Exodus. Actually, there are a number of dates proposed by scholars of varied stripes for the Exodus, but I focus on the two leading dates. According to 1 Kings 6:1, Solomon "began to build the house of the LORD" in the 4th year of his reign, or 967 BCE, which was 480 years after the Exodus. Using this information, the Exodus would have occurred in 1446 BCE, two centuries earlier than the dating generally accepted by scholars in the field. The 480 years mentioned is actually 40 times 12, that is, 12 generations of 40 years each. However, throughout the Bible, 40 years isn't always a generation. Sometimes a generation is 20, 30, 70 or even 120 years. Thus, as already stated, I go along with the consensus date of 1250 BCE, or thereabouts, for the Exodus.

Nevertheless, there is a problem with the 1250 dating – if we insist that the author's use of 40 years means 40 calendar years. As already mentioned, the biblical timeline I'm following has Moses being born in 1330, which would be during the reign of Tutankhamun (1341–1323). But as you will see in a moment, Moses' birth would have occurred during the 11-year reign of Seti I (1290–1279).

Then again, an actual generation is closer to 25 years; so the interval from Solomon's fourth year to the Exodus would be 12 x 25 = 300 years. Adding this number to Solomon's fourth year, 967 BCE, gives us the year 1267 BCE, which is in the middle part of the 13th century and during Rameses ll's reign.

Trying to date the Exodus is a will-o'-the-wisp. It's "where archeological interpretation and biblical narrative collide," as biblical scholar Michael D. Oblath put it. Egyptologist Kenneth Kitchen, with fence-sitting owlishness, adds: "…a 13th-century exodus remains – at present – the *least objectionable* (my italics) dating."

So it's the 13th century BCE (until further notice). But what an interesting time it was. Seti 1 was on the throne from 1290–1279 BCE shortly after the start the century, and he seems to have shuttled back and forth between Memphis, the capital, just a few miles south of Cairo, and the Delta between the Tanitic and Pelusiac distributaries, some 60 miles north, where he had plans to relocate the capital.

"And they built for Pharaoh treasure cities,[34] Pithom and Raamses" (Exodus 1:11, KJV). Pithom, located east of the Pelusiac, was primarily a grainary. Rameses contained two buildings that served as storehouses for threshed grain, but Seti was planning a large city, which he and his son, Ramesses 11, would build.

The Hebrews in bondage, about 20,000 (not 2 million, as so many are taught) of them in Goshen, were Pharaoh's main work force, no doubt supplemented by prisoners of war – Nubians, Libyans, Asiatics – and others who were sold into slavery. The king didn't appreciate Moses and Aaron's chutzpah in telling him to let the people go ("three days' journey into the desert, and sacrifice unto the LORD our God"). His response, in Exodus 5:7 was: "Ye [his officers] shall no more give the people straw to make brick, as heretofore: let them go and gather straw for themselves."

The Exodus material about brick making rings true. Making mud bricks with straw is documented in ancient Egyptian records, such as papyruses Anastasi III and IV from the Ramesside period.[35] A document dealing with brick making, the Lourve Leather Roll, dated to Year 5 of Ramesses 11, cites brick production targets and then the number of bricks actually delivered. For instance, Yupa

---

34   The NIV has it as store cities and the New Living Translation as "supply cities for the king."

35   For the eleven pharaohs who took the name Ramesses (1292–1069 BCE).

son of Urhiya, a trainee stable-master in Ramesses ll's Great Stable,[36] at one stage in his training program was to make 2000 bricks but delivered 1630, with a deficit of 370. Yupa, from a well-established and wealthy family, started at the bottom and worked his way up in what was a tolerant society, becoming High Steward of the king and then Steward of the Ramesseum (Ramesses' cult temple). Egyptian records actually have a great deal to say about him and his illustrious father, Urhiya. I found reading about their lives in these ancient documents made the 13th century BCE come alive.

Year 5 of Ramesses ll's reign, 1274 BCE, was a memorable year. It was the year Ramesses went to war against the Hittite Empire under its king, Muwatalli ll. History records their clash as the Battle of Kadesh, also known as the War for Canaan, the ancient world's most thoroughly documented military face-off.

As already mentioned, Seti 1 was busy commuting between Memphis and the Nile Delta, preparing to build a new capital, the royal city of Pi-Ramesses (meaning "House of Ramesses") at what is today Qantir, close to the ruins of the old Hyksos capital, Avaris. Commerce was booming all around the Mediterranean rim, and he wanted to be closer to Egypt's ports. Another reason given for his desire to relocate his capital was his wish to get away from the influence of the powerful Amun priesthood entrenched in Thebes. A third reason was the most logical: the move was in response to Muwatalli's chess-board relocation of his court closer to the Mediterranean. Ramesses ll felt he had to counter Muwatalli's tactic.

The Egyptian Empire and the Hittite Empire were the two superpowers of the early 13th century BCE, and it was only a matter of time before they clashed. A note of explanation, the Hittites

---

36   Held as many as 460 horses.

were an ancient Anatolian people who established an empire around 1600 BCE in a large area of Asia Minor or what is today Turkey. Their empire had its capital in Hattusa[37] (also spelled Hattusha) in the north-central part of the country. Muwatalli moved the royal seat to the Bronze Age city of Tarhuntassa, located to the south and closer to the sea.

What touched off the war was the conflict over who would control the kingdom of Amurru, which stretched from the northern coast of what is today Lebanon into central Syria. Amurru was the empire of the Amorites, an ancient Semitic people from Syria. In the Hebrew Bible, they are mentioned as living in or near Canaan since the time of Abraham.

And so one day in the spring of 1274 BCE, Ramesses ll, known to Egyptians as *Userma'atre'setepenre*, "Keeper of Harmony and Balance, Strong in Right, Elect of Ra," and Muwatalli ll, the chosen of the Luwian[38] weather god Tarhunt, his heavenly bodyguard, squared off outside of Kadesh on the Orontes River north of Damascus near the Lebanese-Syrian border, on the Syrian side, in the largest chariot battle ever fought.

There had been a major chariot battle about two hundred years earlier at Megiddo. In the 15th century BCE, Egyptian forces under Pharaoh Thutmose lll had conquered Kadesh. That campaign followed his victory 8 years earlier at the Battle of Megiddo in 1457 BCE against a rebellious coalition of Canaanite city-states led by King Durusha of Kadesh and the king of Megiddo. In the 14th century BCE, the Hittite king, Suppiluliuma 1 (reigned c. 1344–1322 BCE), an expansionist ruler like Ramesses ll, retook Kadesh.

---

37   Settlements in the Hattusa area date back to the 6th millennium BCE.

38   The Luwians were Bronze Age and early Iron Age Indo-European people from western Asia Minor and the northwestern Levant.

Ramesses had to wait until the omens were auspicious before he could launch his war machine against the Hittites. Finally, having propitiated the gods with sufficient sacrifices, the priests said the time was right and he left Pi-Ramesses in March or April of 1274 BCE with 2000 chariots and an army of 20,000 men split into four equally divided corps named after the four dominant gods of Egypt: Amun, Ra, Ptah, and Set. Ramesses himself was at the head of the Amun division: 4000 foot soldiers and about 500 chariots each containing 2 charioteers.

As Ramesses and his forces neared Kadesh, he came upon two Shasu[39] Bedouins who told him that the Hittite king and his army were way up north in Aleppo, too frightened to engage the mighty king of Egypt. But then his scouts arrived with two Hittite prisoners who, with a little persuasion, confessed that Muwatalli and his entire army were close by. We might say just over the nearest sand dune.

While Ramesses was pondering the situation with his princes, Muwatalli's chariots slammed into the Ra division as it was making its way toward his headquarters. The Battle of Kadesh would be a 13th century BCE equivalent of a World War ll tank battle between light, highly mobile M4 Shermans with their 75-millimeter guns and the dreaded, heavy-plated but slow-moving German 54-ton-Tigers armed with formidable 88 mm. guns. Mawatalli had the equivalent of the Tiger tanks.

The Hittite king and his allies had somewhere between 23,000 and 50,000 men and anywhere from 2500 to 3700 chariots. He had 19 allies, including Sattuara of Mitanni, Niqmepa of

---

39   Ancient Egyptians referred to Bedouin shepherds as "Shasu" (those who traveled on foot). An inscription from the time of Amenhotep lll mentions "the Shasu of YHW." How the Shasu may fit into the history of the Hebrews in Egypt is beyond the scope of this book.

Ugarit, Niqmaddu of Kadesh, Talmi-Sarruma of Aleppo, and Mittanamuwash of Pitassa. Their chariots were larger and heavier than Ramesses' and carried three charioteers. These war wagons devastated the Ra division and then Ramesses' Amun division as they rammed through the enemy lines. But they lacked maneuverability, and this is where the lighter, faster Egyptian chariots were able subsequently to out-maneuver and out-fight their counterparts.

Only the two mentioned divisions, Ra and Amun, were engaged in the battle against Muwatalli's superior forces. Through bold fighting, cool-headedness, and what amounted to a display of considerable personal courage was Ramesses able to extricate himself from the difficult position he was in. Both sides declared victory, Ramesses in an elaborate inscription in hieroglyphics, and Muwatalli in his own inscription in cuneiform. Historians declare the Battle of Kadesh a draw. Ramesses had managed to escape with his army still intact, although he suffered heavy casualties, and Muwatalli, also licking his wounds, could boast that his foe failed to capture Kadesh.

About 15 years after the battle, 1259 BCE (some sources give the year as 1258), Ramesses ll and Hattusilis lll signed the Treaty of Kadesh, the world's first documented peace treaty. Muwatalli had died in 1272 BCE and was succeeded by his eldest surviving son, Mursili lll, who was dethroned by his uncle, Hattusilis, in 1265 BCE.

CHAPTER 6

News of the great battle between Ramesses and Muwatalli reached Moses, now 57 and a Midianite shepherd, some months later. Ever since coming to Midian 17 years earlier, he had been living with his Midianite wife Zipporah and his son Gershom in Madian, located about 75 miles south of the tip of the Gulf of Aqaba off its eastern shore. His wife's father, Jethro, was the chief priest of Midian and a pastoralist, who introduced the erstwhile Egyptian prince to the life of shepherdry.

Moses retained a keen interest in events in Egypt, and caravans coming from the Nile Delta or Memphis kept him up to date as to what was happening in *Om El Donya*.[40] A caravan carrying spices and a variety of luxury goods en route from Pi-Ramesses to northwestern Arabia on the Incense Road paused in Madian in September or October of 1274 BCE, and Moses and his father-in-law were up late that night discussing what they had heard about the war between Egypt and Hatti[41] from caravan travelers. As he prepared to go to bed, his mind summarized what he was able to piece together. He grasped that neither army had won a decisive victory. But the significance of the battle went beyond what happened on the battlefield. The crucial point was that Tarhunt, one of the supreme gods of the Hittites, had fought the great god of

---

40 Ancient Egypt was known as the "Mother of the World." The Greek historian Herodotus called Egypt "the gift of the Nile." During the Old Kingdom (2686–2134 BCE), Egypt was known as Kemet, or simply Kmt, meaning "the black land," referring to the rich soil of the Nile Valley. The Hebrew for Egypt is Mitsrayim. The Egyptians were Hamites, descended from Ham, one of Noah's sons.

41 The name for the country of the Hittites.

Egypt, Amun-Ra,[42] to a standstill. Moses muttered: "Amun-Ra, worshipped throughout Egypt, is not invincible, after all. Hmm. That's something to remember."

Well, when we had last encountered the baby Moses in these pages, he was three years old and recently weaned. It was time for Yochebed to surrender her child to the woman identified as Pharaoh's daughter, who had claimed him as a three-month-old infant. How Yochebed handled the emotional trauma of the dissociation of the mother-child dyadic bond is something the author of Exodus does not deal with. We, reading the story, can say we feel her anguish. But for all we know, she might have felt relieved to know that her son was in good hands with a promising future. However, what probably gnawed at her core was the disconcerting thought he would grow up worshipping pagan gods and would not know the god of his ancestors, El Shaddai. Of course, I'm sitting here with my 21st century mind putting thoughts into the mind of a 13th-century BCE mother. *Non est sapientem.* ("It's not wise.")

As noted earlier, we have already met five main characters in chapter 2 of Exodus: repeating myself, the three-month old infant, his Levite parents and sister, and Pharaoh's daughter, whom I refer to as "the princess." The first of these to be named is the three-year-old: "And she called his name Moses: and she said, Because I drew him out of the water" (Ex. 2:10). In Hebrew, his name is Moshe, derived from *mashah*, "drew out" (as from the water), that is, saved from the water. But the princess named him in her maternal language, and in Egyptian the root *mse* or *mos* means "child of" as in Thutmose ("child of the god Thoth") and Ramesses ("child of the sun god Ra"). Thus, "Moses" is half a name.

---

42 Amun (or Amon) was the "King of the Gods." He became joined with the sun god Ra (or Re), to become Amun-Ra, the "one-one."

Because she drew him out of the waters of the Nile, the princess may have named him for the Nile god, the popular Hapi, bringer of water and fertility.[43] Moses' full name, in that case, would have been Hapmose. Eighty years later at the burning bush in Midian, where God, as El Shaddai, brings him back to his Hebrew roots (Exodus 3:6), he drops the front-end of his name, which is a pagan god's name, now to be shunned. But I'm getting ahead of the story.

I need to interject here something I mentioned above but left dangling. There's a bit of information from the opening verses of the Book of Exodus that concerns the infant's parents which needs to be emphasized: they are both Levites. The Levites were the priestly tribe among the Hebrews, who had been in bondage ever since "there arose up a new king over Egypt, which knew not Joseph" (Exodus 1:8). Joseph was brought to Egypt as a slave during the time of the Hyksos kings. The Hyksos were a mixed Semitic people from the northern Levant – Lebanon and Syria – or they could have been of Canaanite origin – who conquered the eastern Nile Delta some time before 1650 BCE and ruled for more than one hundred years. Egyptologists date the arrival of Joseph in Egypt to about 1650 BCE, perhaps even a bit earlier. If the Hebrew tribes were in the Nile Delta for 430 years, as the story goes, that would take us down to about 1260 BCE, close to one of the dates proposed for the Exodus (q.v.).

Thus far only the three-month-old infant from among the five characters introduced in the opening verses of chapter 2 of Exodus has been named,[44] and the next to be named will be the princess, who is identified as the enigmatic daughter of Pharaoh.

---

43 Actually, god of the annual flooding of the Nile, not the god of the Nile itself.

44 We never do learn what Amram and Yochebed called their child while he was with them for the first three years of his life.

But which pharaoh? The consensus among biblical scholars is that he was Seti I, son of Rameses 1 and father of Rameses ll, and the reigning pharaoh (1290–1279 BCE). The princess is not named until 1 Chronicles 4:18, when "the Chronicler" refers to her as Bithiah (lit. "daughter of Yah," Yah being a shortened form of YHVH). The authorship of Chronicles is dated to 350–300 BCE, which would be about a thousand years after the Exodus. By that time, there was no one in the authors' scriptorium in Jerusalem who knew Egyptian; so she was given a Hebrew name. Later the 1st-century Jewish historian Flavius Josephus, writing in Rome after the first Jewish war against Rome, did give her an Egyptian name, Thermuthis,[45] in his *Antiquities of the Jews.*

There are those among the scholars who see a similarity in the names Thermuthis and Thutmose. (I, for one, don't. But what do I know!) If you add 80, Moses' age at the time of the Exodus, to 1446 BCE, the other most popular date proposed for the event, you arrive at the year 1526 BCE, which would be the year of Moses' birth. That would have been in the middle of Pharaoh Thutmose l's reign (1539–1514 BCE). Thutmose and his wife Ahmose had one child, a daughter named Hatshepsut. Some writers in the field identify Hatshepsut as the "Pharaoh's daughter" who rescued the baby Moses and subsequently went on to become a powerful ruler over all of Egypt. (I don't get excited over this morsel of information; I just threw it in to be thorough.)

In Exodus 2:5, we read that "the daughter of Pharaoh came down to wash herself at the river." This was not your typical Saturday night bath but a ceremonial bath. Nearby was a shrine to her god or goddess of fertility, which could have been Amun, the creator-god who was also associated with fertility; Isis, goddess of

---

45   In the 2nd-century BCE Book of Jubilees, Pharaoh's daughter is identified as Tharmuth.

motherhood and fertility; Taweret, goddess of fertility and child-birth, known as the "Lady of the Birth House"; and so on.

Bithiah or Thermuthis , sister of Seti 1, was thought to have been a childless widow, and the one thing she wanted above all else in life was a child; so while she was living in the king's summer palace in the Nile Delta, she prayed at the shrine to her god or goddess for a son. Lo and behold, her praying was answered. When she found the 3-month-old in his water-proof basket, she identified him immediately as "one of the Hebrews' children" (Ex. 2:6), probably from the distinctive design of the swaddling clothes he was wrapped in, but nevertheless embraced him unhesitatingly, ignoring the king's edict, which called for her to drown the infant in the Nile.

Seti, no doubt, was furious when he learned what his sister had done. He could have ordered her death, as well as the Hebrew child's, at that moment. After all, no one defies a royal decree. But Bithiah had an Aladdin's lamp. The child was the gift of her god/goddess, and no one, not even a king, was above the gods.

At some point, which would have been early in his reign, which began in 1290 BCE, Seti and his entourage, including Bithiah and her 3-year-old adopted son, returned to Memphis, the capital and administrative center of the empire. There the young Prince Moses would grow up. However, the Exodus account tells us nothing about his childhood, adolescence, and early adulthood.

Exodus 2:10 relates how Pharaoh's daughter named the child she found, but in the next verse, Moses is presented to us as a grown man. Exodus 2:11 is one of the most extraordinary passages in the Hebrew Bible. In this one verse, which is actually one sentence, Moses goes from age 3 to age 40 without any details about his life being provided. What was he doing during those 37 years?

The British polymath Lina Eckenstein, for one, invented a childhood for Moses in her novel *Tutankh-aten* (1924).[46] There are other so-called sources, although none of them will satisfy the purist's demand for historical accuracy. We can, for instance, go to extra-biblical sources for information about the early life of Moses. The Talmud relates how Seti, now back in the palace in Memphis, was bouncing his 3-year-old nephew on his knee, when Moses suddenly grasped the king's crown from his head. The monarch's advisors read into the act the child's plan to usurp his uncle's throne and recommended he be put to death. Suffice it to say, borrowing one of Charles Dickens' book titles, the youngster revealed he had "great expectations."

According to Flavius Josephus, in Part II, Chapter 10, "How Moses Made War With The Ethiopians," of his *Antiquities of the Jews*, an Ethiopian army had defeated the Egyptians, and in desperation, Pharaoh turned to Moses, now 27, to save his kingdom. Moses and his army outmaneuvered the Ethiopians and made their way to Saba, the capital of Ethiopia, and lay siege to the well-fortified city. Saba was on an island in Upper Nubia (also called Kush and Ethiopia) at the confluence of the Blue Nile and White Nile to form the Nile.

Tharbis, the Cushite princess of Kush, daughter of King Merops, observed Moses from the royal city's ramparts fighting valiantly in the forefront of his army and fell in love with him. She sent her most trusted servant to him offering to "procure the delivering up of the city" if he promised to marry her. In Numbers

---

46 Not at all unusual. Anne Rice, queen of the vampire genre, created a childhood for Jesus in *Christ the Lord: Out of Egypt* (2005). In *The Mummy, or Ramses the Damned* (1990), she resurrected Ramses II for 20th-century horror aficionados.

12:1, Aaron and Miriam criticize Moses for his marriage to a Cushite woman. That woman would be Tharbis.

Luke, in Acts 2:7, writes: "And Moses was learned in all the wisdom of the Egyptians, and was mighty in words and deeds." His defeat of the Ethiopians certainly helps stamp him as mighty in deeds, but the author of Exodus considers Moses less than mighty in words. He describes the hero of Saba as "not eloquent" and "slow of speech" (Ex. 4:10). Public speaking was a valuable aptitude in the ancient world. For instance, in Book IX of the *Iliad*, Phoenix reminds Achilles of the importance of oratorical skill. Odysseus, shrewdest of the Greek commanders, was held in high esteem for his talent as a speaker just as Achilles was for his fighting.

The Talmud provides us with an explanation for Exodus 4:10. When the child Moses grasped Seti's crown, with its shining jewels, from his head, the king's astrologers and counselors saw in this act a threat to Pharaoh's crown and recommended that the child be put to death. One of Seti's advisors suggested that first a test should be conducted to find out if his action was deliberate or if he was simply attracted to the sparkling jewels as any child would be.

Two bowls were placed before the boy, one containing gold and jewels, the other red hot coals. Moses was about to pick up a golden nugget, but an angel maneuvered his hand to a glowing coal, which he put to his lips, burning his tongue in the process. The superstitious king was satisfied that the toddler was harmless. Nevertheless, the incident left Moses with a speech impediment, and he never could become an orator. But from his lips would come the words of the LORD God.

In the Zohar Chadash (The New Zohar), a medieval treatise on Kabbalah, it is said "that, of the ten portions of wisdom that came into the world, the Egyptians had nine, and that all the [other] inhabitants of the earth had only the remaining portion." Egypt was the world's center of learning in the 13th century BCE, and it is assumed that Prince Moses spent his years growing up under the tutelage of some of Egypt's finest minds.

However, we don't learn anything about his early years in Pharaoh's Memphis palace from reading the Book of Exodus. As already stated, the author leaves out 37 years – from ages 3 to 40 – of Moses' life (Exodus 2:11). In Ex. 2:15, he is forced to flee Egypt after coming to the defense of a Hebrew slave being beaten by an Egyptian overseer. Whether he kills the overseer accidentally or deliberately while they struggle is something we don't know. Regardless, the king, who would now be Seti's son, Ramesses ll, issued a death warrant for his "cousin." (Recall, Bithiah was Ramesses aunt, as Seti was Moses' uncle, and, therefore, the two boys were first cousins.)

In Cecil B. DeMille's 1956 screen version of *The Ten Commandments*, Ramesses and an entourage from the court accompany the apprehended Moses to the edge of town. Ramesses doesn't want Moses' blood on his hands and will leave it to the gods to decide his cousin's fate. Provided only a shepherd's staff and a flask of water, Moses must now face a perilous and life-draining desert journey all alone. He survives the hellish desert crossing and winds up in Midian.

The Ten Commandments is movie thaumaturgist DeMille at his best, but he can't resist giving the Book of Exodus the expected Hollywood treatment. More realistically, Moses' wealthy mother, Princess Bithiah, and court friends sequester him in a caravan headed for Midian. He gets off at Madian, 75 miles south of Aqaba on the eastern slope of the Gulf of Aqaba, which is the northeastern extension of the Red Sea. There he encounters the 7 daughters of Jethro and comes to their aid, dispersing a group of bullies who are preventing the girls from watering their sheep at the town's well.

On returning to the family tent, they gleefully report their encounter with the man they call an Egyptian, and Jethro then has his daughters bring Moses to his home. Thus begins the next phase of Moses' life, his 40 years as a Midianite shepherd.

Just as with his treatment of the first 40 years in Egypt, the author tells us little about Moses' life in Midian. He married the eldest of Jethro's daughters, Zipporah, and settled down to a life of looking after woolly ruminants. From a prince of Egypt to a rustic shepherd. With the other national heroes encountered in the great epic tales, the hero usually springs from humble origins and rises to great heights. Moses goes from rags to riches and then from riches back to rags. His story doesn't quite follow the pattern.

Readers of the Book of Exodus are left to ponder why the author furnishes us with so few details about the "early" life of Moses, if 80 years fits the definition of early. Perhaps he just doesn't know much about Moses' life in Egypt and then the supposed equal time he spent in Midian. That's certainly possible. Then again, he may know a good deal about those years of his life but chooses not to divulge what he knows. It seems the author is in a hurry to get to the burning bush, and I can understand and appreciate why. It's because that's where the *real* story of Moses begins.

CHAPTER 7

Where is this land of the Midianites that Moses fled to in the year 1290 BCE? Midian was a region in what is today northwest Arabia. Specifically, it was the land area east of the Gulf of Aqaba, one of the two northern extensions of the Red Sea, and opposite the Sinai Peninsula. To its north were Edom and Moab. In the time of Moses, the term "Arabia" may or may not have included the Sinai Peninsula: the literature is not all that clear concerning Arabia's boundaries. But if Arabia did extend to include Sinai, then, of course, the Sinai Peninsula in the 13th century BCE would be part of what was then Arabia.

This is as good a time as any to introduce the issue of Mount Sinai's actual location. In the 4th century CE, Helena, mother of Constantine the Great, proclaimed Jubal Musa ("the Mountain of Moses") in the Sinai Peninsula to be the biblical Mt. Sinai, which the Christian world then accepted without reservation. Since then, and earlier, a number of locations have been suggested for Mt. Sinai.

Even the apostle Paul, in the first century CE, gets into this discussion. He uses the word "Arabia" in his epistle to the Galatians. Writing allegorically, he says: "For this Agar is mount Sinai in Arabia, and answereth to Jerusalem which now is, and is in bondage with her children" (Galatians 4:25). Hagar,[47] Sarah's handmaiden and mother of Ishmael, is represented as a mountain: "for Mount Hagar is Sinai, which is in Arabia." Interestingly, there is an Arabian tradition that Mount Sinai was called Hagar.

---

47 According to a midrash, Hagar was a princess whom Pharaoh gave to Sarah as a gift.

The implication is that for Paul, Mount Sinai is in Saudi Arabia, not the Sinai. In the Hebrew Bible and New Testament, Arabia is always described as south and east of Palestine, which would be today's Saudi Arabia. The Sinai Peninsula, geographically, is south and west of Palestine. And Midian was in northwestern (Saudi) Arabia.

Midian, however, remains a mystery. Some scholars have put forth the idea that Midian wasn't a defined region on the map but rather a confederation or league of nomadic tribes who ranged from Canaan and Sinai all the way east to Jordan.

The terms "Midianite" and "Ishmaelite" can even cause confusion. Genesis 37:28 (KJV) reads: "Then there passed by Midianites merchantmen; and they [Joseph's brothers]...sold Joseph to the Ishmeelites for twenty pieces of silver...." Here the two tribal names are used interchangeably, but the Midianites and the Ishmaelites were not the same, although they would be considered *mishpucha* {Yiddish for "family"). The Ishmaelites descended from Abraham through Hagar. The Midianites were descendants of Midian, one of the sons of Abraham and his second wife Keturah.

At the beginning of this chapter, I mentioned that Moses fled Egypt for Midian in 1290 BCE. As already noted, the author of Exodus divides Moses' life into three equal parts, each lasting 40 years. If we take 1250 BCE as the year of the Exodus, then Moses departed Egypt in 1290 BCE. Biblical chronology should only be this simple!

The number "40" is mentioned 146 times in the Bible. In Christian numerology, it represents a period of testing, trial, or probation. For Jews, it's not a numerological issue but simply basic Hebrew. Most languages have idiomatic expressions, and in Hebrew, "40 days and 40 nights," means "for some time." As for 40 years, a designation of time that appears frequently enough in the Bible, it can mean "a long time," but then again it can, conceivably, indicate a calendar 40 years. But don't count on that being the case here.

Moses was at the summit of Mt. Sinai for "40 days and 40 nights" (Ex. 24:18). That is, he was up there for some time. Jesus fasted "forty days and forty nights" in the Judean wilderness, where he was tempted by the devil (Matthew 4:1). The verse also states that after his fast, "he was hungry." Starving would be a more accurate description – unless "forty days and forty nights" means "for awhile," which we can interpret as "a few days."

Jesus also went without water for those 40 days and 40 nights. Mahatma Gandhi managed to go three weeks without food in 1924, but no one can go more than a week or so without water.[48] Even a god-man like Jesus fasting in the broiling heat of the desert would succumb to fatal dehydration after a while.

In the Jewish tradition, fasting for the duration of a day was and continues to be the custom. On the Day of Atonement, the holiest day of the year, which sets the standard, Jews are to fast from sundown to sundown, a period of 24 hours (Leviticus 23:27–32). The 40-day-and-40-night fasts of Moses, Elijah (1 Kings 19:8), and Jesus come under the heading of the miraculous and belong more appropriately to the spiritual, not the physical, realm. In the account I'm following, we're in the physical realm.

Getting back to Moses, there is, of course, no way to substantiate that he was born in 1330 BCE, 80 years before the Exodus in 1250 BCE. Once again, as I have been belaboring the point, 40 years in ancient Hebrew thinking doesn't necessarily indicate 40 calendar years. And for that matter, 1250 BCE for the Exodus is still an estimate, a timeline convenience, not a historically fixed date.

---

48   Gandhi did take water, with or without salts and sour limes, during his many protest fasts, 17 in all, as part of India's freedom movement.

As for Moses' hasty exit from Ramses, there were several caravan routes from the Nile Delta to Midian, and it's a matter of speculation as to which one his caravan followed. He could have proceeded from Ramses, where he joined the caravan in disguise, to Succoth and then south-southeast along the eastern shore of the Gulf of Suez to what is the traditional Mount Sinai in the south central part of the peninsula.

In the 13th century BCE, the Sinai was not a part of Egypt proper but was under Egyptian control. It is doubtful if Moses, number one on Pharaoh's Most Wanted List, would have sought a safe harbor in a territory that answered to Memphis, for his cousin's gendarmes would catch up with him sooner or later.

Had he taken this route on his way to Midian, he would have passed through or been close to Serabit el-Khadim and Wadi Magharah in the southwest Sinai Peninsula, where mining for turquoise, a gemstone prized for millennia, was a major occupation. Actually, mining for metals and precious stones in the Sinai dates back to 6000 BCE.

Historian Lina Eckenstein theorized, in *A History of Sinai* (1921), that Serabit el-Khadim was the actual location of Mt. Sinai. The site contains a temple of Hathor, patron goddess of miners, built by Pharaoh Rameses ll. Hathor took many forms, but her most popular iconographic representation was that of a cow. She was also depicted as a woman with cow's ears or a pair of ornate horns. Eckenstein added that Aaron fashioned the golden calf in the temple of Hathor while Moses was on the mountain's summit. (More on the golden calf later.)

This is the second time I have mentioned Lina Eckerstein, historian, prolific author, philosopher, linguist, and early feminist. She is best remembered for her writings on medieval monastic women, especially her *Women Under Monasticism* (1896). Eckerstein was also an amateur archeologist and was part of Egyptologist

Flinders Petrie's team on a number of digs, including Serabit. In addition to *A History of Sinai*, she wrote *The Moon Cult in Sinai* (1911), about Khonsu, the god of the moon.

Worship of Khonsu was at its height during the Ramesside period, the Nineteenth and Twentieth Dynasties (1294–1069 BCE), which was the second half of the New Kingdom (c.1550–c.1077). Memphis was a center of the cult of Khonsu, and we may surmise that Moses growing up in Pharaoh's palace in the capital would have known about the moon god.

There was also a trade route that proceeded east from Ramses past the Bitter Lakes and Nakhl (also spelled Nekhel), ancient capital of the Sinai in the geographic center of the peninsula, to Aqaba, a distance of 225 miles. Caravans with donkeys – camels were not yet domesticated for travel in the 13th century BCE – averaged about 25 miles a day (3 miles per hour for 8 hours). In his *The Northern Hegaz*, the early 20th-century Czech explorer Alois Musil notes that a number of ancient Arab sources mention Moses traveling from Egypt to Madian in Midian, a distance of nine nights' encampments: six nights' encampments from Ramses to the northern tip of the Gulf of Aqaba and then three more to Madian, all in all, 225 miles.

In all probability, this is the route Moses followed. At Aqaba, the caravan turned south and entered Midian. At Haql, 25 miles down and a little inland from the eastern shore of the Gulf of Aqaba, the water was bitter and not fit to drink. The next watering hole, after another 25 miles, was as-Saraf, but no water was available there. The following day brought the caravan to Madian (today's al-Bad'[49]), 75 miles from Aqaba, where there was plenty

---

49   In his *Fire on the Mountain: Geography, Geology and Theophany at Jabal al-Lawz*, geographer Glen A. Fritz relates that when he was exploring the region, he was not permitted to stop in Al-Bad' (modern

of refreshing water, and this was where Moses got off. The rest is, as they say, history. However, remember, thus far in this account, it can be said that the boundary between history and storytelling is somewhat ambiguous.

"And the shepherds [local bullies] came and drove them away [Jethro's sheep at the well]: but Moses stood up and helped them [Jethro's seven daughters]...." (Ex. 2:17). Perhaps there were three or four, or even six town hooligans. The number wouldn't matter. Moses had been a military man, a general, who had fought fearlessly and ferociously in the forefront of his Egyptian army at Saba and more recently had killed one of Pharaoh's slave masters with his bare hands. Now, when he flashed his Khopesh,[50] the bullies fled.

Jethro, "the priest of Midian" (Ex. 3:1) and a Kenite shepherd, welcomed Moses with open arms, and soon enough Moses married his patron's eldest daughter, Zipporah. They had two sons, Gershom and Eliezer (who, apparently, was born late in Moses' sojourn in Madian). Names cannot be divorced from their meaning in the biblical tradition. Gershom is usually explained to mean "a sojourner there," a reference to Moses' flight from Egypt and the refuge he found in Midian: "...for he said, I have been an alien in a strange land" (Ex. 18:3). "And the name of the other was Eliezer...." (Ex. 18:4), the name meaning "God is my help." Benson's Commentary[51] points out that it would be better to translate the passage as, "The Lord is my help, and will deliver me." Benson ends the sentence with, "from the sword of Pharaoh." In other words, Moses feared Ramesses would still try to kill him

---

    Madiam, Moses' home during his years living in Midian). The Saudi
    authorities explained that "it is a Jewish area and is off limits."

50   Bronze scimitar-shaped sword.

51   Joseph Benson (1749–1821), an early English Methodist minister.

when he returned to Egypt to free his people. This is contradictory to Ex. 4:19 (KJV): "And the LORD said unto Moses in Midian, Go, return unto Egypt: for all the men are dead which sought thy life." But now I'm wandering and getting ahead of the story.

Jethro, Moses' father-in-law, is something of a mystery man in the Bible. In Hebrew, the name is *Yitro*, derived from the word *yeter* meaning "abundance." He is also referred to as Reuel, which may have been a given name, and Jethro was a title, such as "Excellency." In Exodus 3:1, Jethro is described as "the priest of Midian," not as a_priest of Midian, indicating he may have been the chief priest, along the lines of, say, a bishop in the Catholic Church.

Reuel literally means a "friend of El," that is, "friend of God." El (spelled *aleph-lamed* in Hebrew) was the supreme god in the Canaanite pantheon, and Abraham was certainly familiar with the name. The god he worshipped when he lived in Ur and Haran before settling in Canaan has yet to be named.

The Canaanites venerated their dead and transmuted them into household gods and goddesses, referred to as the Elohim, which is the plural of El. Another interpretation, in the hierarchical organization of the Canaanite pantheon, the god El when pluralized as Elohim was at the very apex as the "god of gods." The ancient Hebrews came up with a number of names for their god, including the Canaanite Elohim. Early Christian theorists saw in the plurality of the name an opening to interject their trinitarian concept of God – God the Father, God the Son, and God the Holy Spirit.

The ternary godhead is a non-Jewish concept and incompatible with Judaic thought. Who came up with this intriguing idea for nascent Christianity in the 1st century? Whoever he was – a pagan convert to the Jesus movement? – he may have had in mind the Capitoline Triad of Jupiter, king of the gods; Juno, his wife and sister; and Minerva, goddess of wisdom,[52] worshipped through-out the empire and principally in an ornate temple on Rome's Capitoline Hill during the time of the Julio-Claudian dynasty (Augustus to Nero, 27 BCE--68 CE).

Early Christianity was competing with a variety of cults for adherents. Three gods compressed into one might appeal to poly-theists as an alternative to the burdensome necessity of worship-ping three distinct deities. The fact that the Christian triad did not include a feminine representation would at least intrigue Rome's male population in what was a masculinist society.

Abraham also knew God as El Shaddai ("God Almighty"). In Exodus 6:3, God says: "And I appeared unto Abraham, unto Isaac, and unto Jacob, by *the name of* God Almighty [El Shaddai], but by my name JEHOVAH [Yahweh] was I not known to them."

We find God mentioned by more than one name in quite a few biblical passages. "That they may know that You alone, whose name is the LORD [Yahweh], Are the Most High [El Elyon] over all the earth" (Psalm 83:18).

El also appears as the compound name El Elyon, God Most High, as just illustrated and in a number of other passages. After rescuing his nephew Lot from Kedorlaomer, king of Elam, and the kings allied with him (Gen. 14:15), Abram met Melchizedek, king of Salem and priest of God Most High (El Elyon), the same God Abram worshipped – in contrast to those who worshipped the Canaanite gods.

---

52   Which derived from the earlier Etruscan trio of Tinia, the supreme god, Uni, also Uni-Astre (from Canaanite and Phoenician Ashtart), his wife, and Menerva, their daughter and goddess of wisdom, who displaced a still earlier Archaic Triad of Jupiter, Mars, and Quirinus.

After a spell of madness, Nebuchadnezzer[53] (king of the Neo-Babylonian Empire, 605–562 BCE), was restored to normal mental functioning, for which he "blessed the most High [El Elyon], and I praised and honored him that liveth for ever, whose dominion is an everlasting dominion, and his kingdom is from generation to generation" (Daniel 4:34).

Psalm 18:13 is another illustration while making use of synonymous parallelism: "The LORD [Yahweh] also thundered in the heavens,/And the Most High [El Elyon] uttered His voice."

When all was said and done, that is, when the Hebrew Bible was canonized, God's identity became clear: "I am the LORD [Yahweh], that is My name…." (Isaiah 42:8).

CHAPTER 8

There is not much more to add to Moses' sojourn in Madiam (variant spelling of Madian), except that he passed his time as a shepherd looking after his father-in-law's and his own flock of sheep for forty years. In this instance, I have spelled out "forty" rather than use numerals, because "40" would mean 40. As already pointed out, what can be said is that he lived there for some time, or we might even say for a long time, another expression that is as clear as dirty dishwater.

---

53   In Akkadian, Nabu-kudurri-uzur. Nabu (Nebo in the Bible), son of the god Marduk, was the patron god of scribes, literacy, and wisdom.

Madian, or al-Bad', its modern name, is about 15 miles inland from the Gulf of Aqaba. In the summertime, the weather is stifling, and the local shepherds in the time of Moses took their flocks east into the Hisma high ground, past the Shifa, an area of granite mountains. The first leg of the trek was south about thirty miles to Ainuna (also spelled Aynunah), an oasis bordered by tall palm trees, on the eastern shore of the Red Sea. This was a continuation of the trade route Moses' caravan was traveling before he disembarked at Madian. The trade route continued down the Tihama, the region hugging the Red Sea all the way down to the Bab el Mandeb Strait that connects the Red Sea to the Gulf of Aden. Less than twenty miles south of Ainuna (Elim in the Book of Exodus) the shepherds turned east into Wadi[54] Tiryam, which continued southeast as Wadi Sadr in the Shifa. For Moses, it was another sixty miles to the volcanic lava field known as Harrat Uwayrid in the Hisma, and that was where he would spend several months out of the year with his sheep.

Most likely, Zipporah and Gershom accompanied him, along with a few servants. The Exodus text has little to say about Moses' two sons and even less about the younger of the two, who is not mentioned until Moses is on his way back to Goshen after receiving his commission from God to free his brethren: "And Moses took his wife and his sons, and set them upon an ass, and he returned to the land of Egypt...." (Exodus 4:20).

Not until Ex. 18:4 does the author reveal the name of Moses' second son: "And the name of the other was Eliezer; for the God of my father, said he, was mine help, and delivered me from the sword of Pharaoh."(Etymologically, Eliezer is derived from *Eli*, my God + *ezer*, help.) There is no mention of Eliezer's birth in the

---

54   A channel or riverbed that is dry except in the rainy season.

text, and he seems to have arrived on the scene late in his father's forty years in Midian.

The family trek from Madiam to the Harrat lava field region was an annual event. The first year Jethro showed Moses the way, which was relatively easy until they got into the Shifa mountains. To this day, no one knows the approach they then took the rest of the way, although a likely path can be figured out – and has been by Colin Humphreys. (See his *The Miracles of Exodus*).

After Moses' year of what I will call his apprenticeship in shepherding, Jethro was satisfied his son-in-law could manage the family sheep business, freeing him to devote more time to traveling about Midian in his role as chief priest. The text repeatedly tells us he was a Midianite priest, but says nothing about which Midianite god he served.

Moses, now in charge, led the sheep to the Harrat area another thirty-nine times, and then, in his fortieth year as a Midianite shepherd, something happened that would dramatically change his life – and history. He came upon a bush that appeared to be burning without being consumed. Actually, he had witnessed the same phenomenon in that area of Midian on a number of occasions. But this time something else happened. He heard a voice emanating from the bush on fire saying: "Take off your sandals, for you are on holy ground."

Instinctively, he understood he was hearing the voice of a god, which, naturally, he took to be that of the Midianite god he had been worshipping for forty years, the god Zipporah and her sisters worshipped, the god of Gershom, and the god his father-in-law served. As for the language of the voice he heard, it spoke to him in Proto-Arabic, the language of Midian.

The next thing Moses heard was the voice saying: "I am the God of your father...." (Ex. 3:6). He was perplexed and confused, until he realized it was not the voice of his local Midianite god but the voice of the god of his father, Amram. Immediately, the voice continued, reinforcing the previous utterance and completing the sentence, with: "…the God of Abraham, the God of Isaac, and the God of Jacob."

Moses was overwhelmed. The text says he "hid his face; for he was afraid to look upon God." Once he regained his composure, he spent hours, probably days, even longer, reflecting on the meaning of his encounter with the God of his fathers. He was, indisputably, a **Hebrew** and not an Egyptian, that is, not an Egyptian by blood. In our own terminology, he would be considered an Egyptian Hebrew, in the same sense that Jews living in the United States are American Jews or Jewish Americans.

The text is parsimonious with words. So much is left to the imagination when it comes to trying to fill in details. We do not know, for instance, if Moses was concerned with identity issues as so many of us are today. He may have grown up as an Egyptian prince living in a palace, but he was aware he was a Hebrew whose parents were Hebrews in Goshen. We have no way of knowing if, at any stage of his life including his years in Midian, he struggled with identity.

It was the child psychoanalyst Erik Erikson who gave us the concept of the "identity crisis" with his book *Identity, Youth and Crisis* (1968). A prime example of an adolescent with an identity crisis would be the young Barack Hussein Obama. Half white and half black, he struggled, internally, with the identity issue, until he resolved his conflict. He would live as a black man.

Obama's adolescent conflict ran deeper than that: he was also conflicted when it came to religion. His mother, Stanley Ann Dunham, raised as a Christian, married Kenyan Muslim Barack Hussein Obama, Sr. in 1961. The former president was born that year. His parents divorced in 1964, and Ann Dunham married Indonesian Muslim Lolo Soetoro the following year. As a child,

Barack Hussein Obama, Jr. spent several formative years in Jakarta.[55] How he resolved his Christian- Muslim issue is a matter that goes beyond the scope of this work.

Was Moses bothered by an identity problem as a youth or during those years in the Midian desert? It's an intriguing question. The mind of 13th-century BCE man was not like ours, at least according to psychologist Julian Jaynes, who developed the right brain/left brain theory, explained in his book *The Rise of Consciousness in the Breakdown of the Bicameral Mind* (1976).[56]

In Jaynes' bicameral (two chambers) concept, ancient man had not as yet developed introspection and self-awareness, that is, consciousness. He defined consciousness `simply as "that which is introspectable." Introspection, as defined in psychology, is the examination of one's conscious thoughts and feelings.

In bicameralism, the right cerebral hemisphere *speaks* – hallucinates a voice,; that is, a god issues commands and advice –and the left cerebral hemisphere obeys unquestioningly. Schizophrenic command hallucinations may be considered a residue of the bicameral brain. Bicamerality, Jaynes states, existed until as recently as 3000 years ago. Moses lived in the time of bicameral man and as such would have lacked the capacity for introspection. In all likelihood, he would not have been capable of experiencing an identity crisis.

The human brain was a rudimentary structure in archaic man. It would "grow" – develop more and more interneuronal

---

55   Although Indonesia is a Sunni Muslim country, the Soetoros lived in a section of Jakarta that is Shiite. Just for the record, Iran is a Shiite country.

56   For those who find they don't have the time to do much reading, there is a short chapter summarizing Jaynes' book in my *Journey's End: The Name.*

connections – with time. But in Moses' time, it was still a primitive, pre-conscious organ. He would not have been capable of analyzing the Battle of Kadesh as I had him doing in chapter 6 – *unless* he was at an early stage of transitioning from bicameral status to conscious thinking.

CHAPTER 9

N ow comes the challenge. God says to Moses: "Come now therefore, and I will send thee unto Pharaoh, that thou mayest bring forth my people the children of Israel out of Egypt" (Ex. 3:10). Moses, however, balks at accepting the divine commission offered him. He comes up with excuses, including a speech impediment that dates back to his childhood days in Pharaoh's palace when he burned his mouth with a hot coal: "…I am slow of speech, and of a slow tongue" (Ex. 4:10).

The God of Abraham, Isaac, and Jacob is incensed: "And the anger of the LORD was kindled against Moses, and he said, Is not Aaron the Levite thy brother? I know that he can speak well…" (Ex. 4:14). This is the first time Aaron, who is three years older than Moses,[57] is mentioned. He will play a key role in the Exodus drama, more so than what is included in the text.

According to Maimonides, the medieval Jewish sage, the patriarch Jacob appointed his son Levi to teach the people the ways of

---

57 "And Moses was fourscore years old, and Aaron fourscore and three years old, when they spake unto Pharaoh" (Exodus 7:7).

serving God. Amram, the son of Kohath and grandson of Levi, became the spiritual head, that is, priest, of the tribes after his father's death. Aaron, the firstborn son of Amram, assumed the mantle with Amram's death. The firstborn son was considered the appropriate "emissary of the congregation."

In the above Exodus quote, LORD is spelled in caps, which is the accepted English equivalent of the Hebrew Tetragrammaton, YHVH, or Yahweh when vowels are added. Yahweh would eventually, in the 12th century CE, evolve into the hybrid word Jehovah (in Christianity). The name of God, YHVH, was considered too holy to be pronounced in antiquity; so the term *Adonai*, meaning "My Lord," was substituted, and several other terms for God came into use as well, such as *HaShem* ("The Name"), the Ancient of Days (Book of Daniel), *Shamayim* (which is also the Hebrew for heaven), et cetera.

Moses, conqueror of the unassailable city of Saba, capital of Ethiopia, in his younger years, nevertheless felt honored to hear El Shaddai's offer to free his people in bondage, reviving as it did memories of past glory as a military commander for Pharaoh, but he did not jump at what could be considered the opportunity of a lifetime. He equivocated, while he tried to figure out how to reject God's commission without angering Him. In the world in which he lived, he understood, as did everyone, that it was perilous to anger the gods.

The dialoging between Moses and God concerning the mission is contained in chapters 3 and 4 of Exodus. The account is considerably condensed, with most of what was germane left out. Furthermore, the fourth-century BCE redactor, in preparing the version we have of Exodus, may or may not have followed

Moses' original urtext.[58] This provocative statement will become understandable in due course. (At least, I hope it will.)

Moses had good reason to doubt that the goal was achievable. He did believe he could raise an army to challenge Pharaoh's. But he remembered only too well the outcome of the Battle of Kadesh in the fifth year of Ramesses ll's reign (1274 BCE). Two preeminent gods, the most powerful of all the gods, the Hittite's Tarhunt, and Egypt's Amun-Ra, not just their representative armies, had clashed in a titanic struggle which had ended in a standstill.

Moses couldn't begin to compare El Shaddai to Tarhunt, the god of thunder and slayer of the dragon Illuyanka, whom he had learned about while growing up as Prince Moses, let alone compare him to Amun-Ra, the god he worshipped for most of the first half of his life in Egypt. He thought of El Shaddai as amazingly peripatetic, but a minor god and even an effete god, who had allowed his Hebrew worshippers to endure slavery for countless generations. Strategically, thinking as a field commander, he thought it possible to defeat Ramesses on the battlefield, but El Shaddai was no match against Amon-Ra. The undertaking the God of his father Amram proposed was doomed to fail.

You have to bear this in mind. There was no waiting room filled with applicants for the job. El Shaddai had chosen Moses for the mission, and He was not considering anyone else. His task now was to convince Moses that the undertaking could be realized. In order to do that, El Shaddai would have to explain to the former prince of Egypt just who *He* actually was.

In chapter 4, I had mentioned one of the Egyptologist Jan Assmann's books, *Moses the Egyptian: The Memory of Egypt in Western Monotheism*. The title, *Moses the Egyptian*, warrants our

---

58   Tradition ascribes authorship of the Torah to Moses. Urtext is the original or earliest version of a text.

attention. By 1998, when the book came out, there was no hullaba-loo over the title. But that was not the case in 1939 when Sigmund Freud published his historical novel *Moses and Monotheism*. Freud created an international uproar in religious, academic and lay circles with his polemic by portraying Moses as having been born an Egyptian, in addition to being reared as one. He was not the first to suggest this. The American archeologist, Egyptologist and historian James Henry Breasted (*Development of Religion and Thought in Ancient Egypt*) [1912]) and the British Egyptologist as well as journalist Arthur Weigall (*The Life and Times of* Akhnaton) [1910] were on the same wavelength. In fact, these early Ikhnaton researchers were key sources for Freud's *Moses and Monotheism*. In brief, there is an Egyptian connection, a vital one, and it will be the subject of the next chapter.

CHAPTER 10

He has been called history's first modern human. His name was Akhenaten, and he ruled Egypt for 17 years (1353–1336 BCE). Queen Nefertiti, the most celebrated of all ancient Egyptian women, after Cleopatra, was his wife; and perhaps the most famous of the pharaohs, Tutankhamun, was his son (by a second-ary wife). For the first five years of his reign, he was known as Amenhotep 1V.

The name Akhenaten – aso spelled Akhenaton, Ikhnaton and Echnaton – translates as "Effective for Aten" and also as "Horizon of the Aten," and Amenhotep has the meaning of "Amun is satisfied." Amun was one of the most powerful and widely worshipped gods of ancient Egypt, and when fused with the sun god Ra, became even more dominant in the lives of Egyptians. Amun-Ra was the "King of Gods" and was worshipped throughout the empire. Only Osiris, god of the underworld and also god of resurrection, rivaled him in popularity.

Ikhnaton caused a religious earthquake by abandoning the traditional polytheism of Egypt for a quasi-monotheistic cult that worshipped the Aten, or sun disk. He was more than a millennium ahead of his time. While he recognized the Aten as the only god, the people he ruled were not ready to give up their gods. In the forefront of the opposition to his revolutionary religious thinking were the powerful Amun priests. After 17 years of Ikhnaton and his Atenism, known as the "Atenist, or Amarna, heresy," they got rid of him!

I need to introduce a note of explanation here concerning the spelling of Akhenaten, which is the usual way the name appears. However, I spell it as "Ikhnaton," hardly used these days but still an accepted alternate spelling. During the Q&A of my lectures, someone would invariably want to know why I refer to Akhenaten as Ikhnaton when everyone else calls him "Akhenaten." My answer would be: "That's the way I learned it in high school in New York back in 1944, when religion wasn't *verboten* in the school system and academic standards were high," and I have stuck with that spelling ever since. In a way, it demonstrates how far we as a society have come in 75 years – a mark of our cultural retrogression.

Ikhnaton moved his capital from Thebes to the city he built and named, Akhetaten (modern-day Amarna), located about 200 miles north of Thebes, which was abandoned after his death, a death generally accepted to have been an assassination. Thebes had been the capital of Egypt when Ikhnaton ascended to the throne, and it was the Amun priests' stronghold: Amun was the patron deity of Thebes.

Amun, separated from Ra, had always been an influential force in Egyptian life, but in the Pyramid texts, a collection of ancient religious writings, the earliest dating back to about 2400 BCE, containing spells and incantations concerned with protecting the entombed pharaohs' remains, he is depicted as a mere fertility god of Thebes, ranked below the war god Montu and the creator god Atum. He began to gain in power during the period of the Middle Kingdom (2040–1782 BCE) and became ascendant during the New Kingdom (1550–1069), the time referred to as the Egyptian Empire, when Egyptian civilization was at its height.

In Egyptian mythology, Amun's origin traces back to the time of Tep Zepi ("First Time"), the golden age when gods ruled the Earth,[59] before "rage or clamour or strife or uproar had come about," as one (unnamed) author expressively added. The description of the gods' arrival on Earth is reminiscent of a passage in Ezekiel: "And I looked, and, behold, a whirlwind came out of the north, a great cloud, and a fire infolding itself, and a brightness was about it…Also out of the midst thereof came the likeness of four living creatures. And this was their appearance; they had the likeness of a man…." (Ezekiel 1:4–5). Ezekiel's vision is a description of the glory of God and has nothing to do with flying saucers and extraterrestrials. What's coming out of the whirlwind from the north isn't a spaceship but Nebuchadnezzar and his army marching on Judah. Lord Byron similarly captures the moment with the opening lines of "The Destruction of Sennacherib": "The Assyrian came down like the wolf on the fold,/ And his cohorts were gleaming in purple and gold…."

---

59   The Middle Kingdom, the 500-year period from c. 1570 to 1070 BCE), is considered the "golden age" of ancient Egyptian literature.

In 1348 BCE, the fifth year in his reign, Amenhotep IV changed his name to Ikhnaton and began openly to worship his one-and-only god, the Aten. In his Atenism, Ikhnaton had deified the disk of the sun, which in ancient Egyptian mythology had been an attribute or expression of the god Ra. There was nothing anthropomorphic (human form) about Ikhnaton's god, who was represented as rays of light emanating from the sun's disk.

Ikhnaten didn't invent Aten, the sun-disk god, who had been known since the time of the 12th dynasty (1991–1778 BCE), where he was mentioned in *The Story of Sinue*, the remarkable narrative by an unknown author described as the "Egyptian Shakespeare." In this apparently fictionalized story, the dead Pharaoh Amenemhat 1 (reigned 1991–1962 BCE) is described as rising as a god to the heavens, where he is united with the sun disk, the solar Aten. (There was a "silver Aten," which referred to the moon-god.) *Sinue*[60] is written in verse and contains themes that parallel the biblical Joseph, Jonah, King David, and the parable of the Prodigal Son.

It could be said that Ikhnaten inherited the Aten from his father, Amenhotep lll, who worshipped him in private with a small circle of Atenists. What Ikhnaten did was to refine the concept of Aten and make Atenism the religion of the empire.

Was his monotheism pure enough to be comparable to our understanding of the Judeo-Christian God? Mirian Lichtheim, the noted Israeli translator of ancient Egyptian texts, in her *Ancient Egyptian Literature*, vol. 2, points out that Ikhnaten's Aten

---

60   *The Story of Sinue* was the inspiration for Finish author Mika Waltari's 1945 historical novel *The Egyptian* and the subsequent 1954 movie version based on his book. The protagonist of *The Egyptian*, set in the time of Ikhnaten, was named Sinue.

is a syncretic[61] god, clearly revealed as such in his "Great Hymn to the Aten," in which *"Re-Herakhym, Shu and Aten* [my italics] are merged into the creator god."

Re-Herakhy, or Ra-Herakhy, in later Egyptian mythology, was a composite god formed by combining Ra and Horus, the son of Osiris and Isis. The name translates literally as "Ra, who is Horus of the Horizons" and may refer to the sun's journey from horizon to horizon.

Shu, a primordial god, was considered a personification of air. In his role or capacity as the air, he was seen as having a cooling, and therefore, calming influence. This linked him with Ma'at,[62] daughter of Ra and the personification of truth and justice.

The British Egyptologist and papyrologist Dominic Montserrat (*Akhenaten: History, Fantasy and Ancient Egypt*) saw the worship of Aten as monolatry (Gk. *monos*, single, plus *latreia*, worship), an interesting word, meaning the *belief* in many gods but the worship of only one. The 19th-century philologist Max Muller coined the term henotheism, easily confused with monolatry, which he defined as "monotheism in principle and polytheism in fact." Henotheism is usually defined as the worship of one god but *turning to other gods* when your god fails to deliver.

Scholars find similarities, in some passages, between Ikhnaten's "Hymn to Aten" and Psalm 104, attributed to a shared literary tradition between ancient Egypt and Israel.[63] For instance, "…O LORD my God, thou art very great…"(Psalm 104:1), parallels the hymn's: "Sole God beside whom there is none." Verse 24: "O

---

61   Syncretism is the combining of different beliefs.

62   To live by the principle of Ma'at (pronounced may-et) was to live in accordance with the highest ethical and moral standards.

63   The poetic form of the "Hymn to Aten" and Psalm 104 is also found throughout ancient Middle East hymnology.

LORD, how manifold are thy works! in wisdom hast thou made them all: the earth is full of thy riches," parallels Ikhnaten's words: "How many are your deeds…You made the earth as you wished, you alone, all peoples, herds, and flocks." Verse 29: "Thou hidest thy face, they are troubled: thou takest away their breath, they die, and return to their dust," has its parallel in: "When you have dawned they live. When you set they die."

Ikhnaten devoted most of his time and energy to worshipping the Aten. It' interesting how Psalm 104:33 sums up his devotion: "I will sing to the LORD [substitute the Aten] as long as I live: I will sing praise to my God while I have my being."

During the time he withdrew to his sanctuary to pray away the hours, his enemies were nibbling away at the boundaries of his empire and also devouring Nubia and Syria. When he did attend to state business, his energy was concentrated on closing down the many temples to the gods throughout the kingdom, especially those of the Amun priests. Here he ran afoul of powerful enemies. The Amun priesthood found its very existence threatened by the edicts of the unorthodox pharaoh. Ikhnaton died in his 17th regnal year, probably at the hands of those same Amun priests. Officially, historians add a question mark after his death.

Atenism died with the death of Ikhnaten, and Egypt returned to its age-old polytheism. But Ikhnaten lives on – in literature, art, music, film.…

Thomas Mann wrote about him in his *Joseph and His Brothers*, as did Egyptian novelist and Nobel laureate in literature Naguib Mahfouz (*Akhenaten, Dweller in Truth*). Philip Glass composed three operas about visionary thinkers: Albert Einstein (*Einstein on the Beach*), Mahatma Gandhi (*Satyagraha*),[64] and Ikhnaten (*Akhnaten*).

---

64 Gandhi's policy of passive political resistance.

In the French animated feature film *La Reine Soleil* ("The Sun Queen") [2007], based on the novel by Christopher Jacq, Amun priests plot to usurp Ikhnaton's throne. So what else is new? What's new is that instead of a hero we have a heroine, Ikhnaten's 14-year-old daughter Akhesia, who, in the grand heroic tradition, will save the empire for her daddy. Maybe in our postmodern world, but not in male-dominated ancient Egypt!

At a conference in 1912, psychoanalyst Karl Abraham read a paper about whether Ikhnaten had suffered from – what was one of Freud's most cherished concepts – an Oedipus complex. Ikhnaten had removed several monuments built by his father, Amenhotep lll, which Abraham considered to be equivalent to a repressed parricidal wish. Jung disagreed passionately. He touted Ikhnaten as a creative and deeply religious man who harbored no hostility toward his father. Freud, visibly anxious, decried ungrateful sons [meaning Jung] wiping out their fathers' heritage [Freud, the father figure]. Emotionally overwhelmed, Freud then fainted. Soon after, Jung left Freud's psychoanalytic group.

Freud was an avowed atheist, but he was as Jewish as they come and would even joke about his Jewishness. He cherished the Hebrew Bible his father had given him for his bar mitzvah, and when in his eighties, his life's work essentially completed, he returned to the Bible with his *Moses and Monotheism*. The religious world rejected it outright and condemned Freud for being anti-biblical. But as Philip Rosenbloom, writing in the September 2003 issue of *Jewish Magazine*, pointed out: "Far from rejecting the validity of the Bible, Freud accepted it, but only as an external manifestation of the inner trauma of the Jewish nation."

As for Carl Gustav Jung, founder of analytical psychology, during a BBC interview in the 1950s he was asked if he believed in God. He responded, "I don't *believe* [my italics] in God, I know!" Subsequently, he expanded on that statement: "I have had the experience of having been gripped by something that is stronger than myself, something that people call God. So, I will never say that I believe that God exists. I must say I know God exists." The quote is in Jung's *The Undiscovered Self* (1957).

Even the Mexican painter Frida Kahlo found space in her artistic vision to include Ikhnaten. She was married to the muralist Diego Rivera, considered the most influential Mexican artist of the 20th century. Frida referred to Rivera and herself as *pareja extraña del país del punto y la raya* (strange couple from the land of dot and line). In her diary, she drew him and herself as Ikhnaten and Nefertiti, portraying the pharaoh with an exaggerated degree of cardiomegaly (enlarged heart), unguiculate (claw-like) ribs hugging his chest, testicles shaped like a brain, and a penis to match his lover's drooping breast, and Nefertiti holding in her arms the baby she could never have.

And, of course, for those addicted to the History channel, there were episodes in its *Ancient Alien* series suggesting that Ikhnaton may have been an extraterrestrial.

I found conflicting assessments of Ikhnaten – he has been called "the heretic priest," "the enemy," "that criminal," "the most infamous pharaoh of ancient Egypt," et cetera, but, on the other hand, James Breasted considered him "the first individual in human history." Elsewhere in these pages, as I have already noted, he has been labeled "the first modern human," which is a more penetrating description.

Jung saw Ikhnaten as a highly creative individual, and that testiculated brain Frida Kahlo drew in her diary harbored a system of thinking not developed in anyone else as yet in the ancient world. He decried all superstition, that is, supernatural causation. For him, there were no demons, devils, fiery dragons from fog-enshrouded lagoons, fairies, ghosts that appeared from out of nowhere, phantoms, and so on. His brain had leaped into the future, and he thought as we do; that is, he had the capacity for secondary-process thinking, or logical reasoning, whereas his contemporaries had not yet progressed beyond primary-process thinking, which is magical thinking, the way children also think. He was no longer bicameral man but had transitioned into a rational, conscious being. Thus, he indeed could be considered the first modern human.

CHAPTER 11

Moses is at the burning bush dialoguing with God, and he will continue to dialogue with God until the end of his life. I observe that readers of Exodus don't seem to see anything odd about this, but they should. From our perspective, he is *hallucinating*; however, in the 13th century BCE, it was all quite normal. Everybody hallucinated.

Perhaps if I delve a little deeper into Julian Jaynes' theory of bicamerality, introduced in chapter 8, the reader will have a better understanding of how ancient man did his thinking. Stated simply, he hallucinated as the means by which he dealt with his realities. Gods controlled the world, and ancient, or archaic, man tuned in to the voices of his gods, for he was unable to think his way through any stressful situation. He did not have ego and he did not introspect. In other words, he lacked a conscious mind. The gods served in place of consciousness.

When Agamemnon robbed Achilles of his mistress in the *Iliad*, a god grabbed Achilles by the hair and warned him not to strike the king, and another god then consoled him over his loss. Near the end of the Trojan War, when Achilles reminded Agamemnon of the event, Agamemnon said it was Zeus, not he, who caused the act: "What could I do? Gods always have their way." Achilles accepted Agamemnon's explanation, since he too obeyed the gods (he hallucinated).

The *Iliad* heroes heard the voices of their gods as clearly as schizophrenics hear their hallucinated voices today. The gods were organizations of the central nervous system, Jaynes maintains. Bicameral man had a god-brain in his right cerebral hemisphere and a rudimentary man-brain on the opposite side. When Zeus ordered Agamemnon to attack before the walls of Troy, the command was perceived in his right hemisphere, which then directed the left hemisphere to act.

The Moses of the Bible is a bicameral man living in the 13th century BCE, which is the tail-end of archaic man's time. However, he does exhibit nascent evidence of consciousness; he has what might be thought of as a narrow channel connecting his right brain to his left brain, where logical thinking begins. The Moses story as we have it in Exodus, with its archaism, may very well be a 13th-century BCE account that has come down to us relatively intact from the original source.

A good deal of the dialogue between God and Moses in chapter 2 of Exodus is missing, either lost in time or never included in the first place. With what we do read, there is a noticeable lack of detail; that is, the writing is just skin and bones. The writing style developed by the ancients was parsimonious, dictated by the fact that the vocabulary of any language at the time was limited, and it wasn't all that easy to obtain writing material: papyrus, parchment, vellum, leather, ink (made from gall-nuts, gum from the acacia tree, water, and magnesium and copper sulfates), honey to thicken the ink mixture, reed pens....

God – as a reminder, still known to the Hebrews as El Shaddai (also El and Elohim) in the 13th century BCE – would remain steadfast in His pursuit of Moses to accept the commission to liberate his people from their bondage. Moses remained firm, and yet tactful, in rejecting El Shaddai's proposed mission. El Shaddai finally succeeded in breaking through his resistance when He said: "I have chosen you, and only you, for when you dwelt among the Egyptians, you had some understanding of what my beloved son Ikhnaten was all about."

Ikhnaten reigned as king from 1353 to 1336 BCE. Efforts were made to wipe out his memory – his monuments and statues were destroyed and his name dropped from the king lists – but his legacy survived. Moses, possibly born in 1330 BCE, might have heard something about him while growing up in the palace in Memphis.

Moses had indeed learned about the late pharaoh's innovative monotheism during his years living in Egypt, but forty years in Midian had dimmed his memory of the rebel king. He was surprised that merely hearing the name of Ikhnaten again would stir up something within his core. He finally did accept God's liberation project but tentatively.

Nevertheless, he was concerned about how he would be received on his return: "And Moses said unto God, Behold, when I come unto the children of Israel, and shall say unto them, The God of *your* fathers hath sent me unto you, and they shall say to me, What is his name? what shall I say unto them?" (Exodus 3:13). I italicized the personal pronoun "your" because Moses, up until his encounter with El Shaddai, was a Midianite pagan, introduced to his true heritage only now at the burning bush; but he was still unfamiliar and insecure with his new identity as a Hebrew.

The response he received would change everything. "And God said unto Moses, I AM THAT I AM…Thus shalt thou say unto the children of Israel, I AM hath sent me unto you" (Ex. 3:14). And for emphasis, He added: "…this is my name for ever, and this is my memorial unto all generations" (Ex. 3:15).

Moses didn't grasp what the LORD God had just said to him. He was preoccupied, thinking that when he went back to Goshen, the elders, who, since the time of Abraham knew God as El Shaddai, a name of Canaanite origin, would ask him for the name of the god who sent him to them. If he answered that "I AM" sent him, he and his mission would be rejected outright, for they would interpret I AM to be a Midianite pagan god.

God interrupted his thoughts by interjecting, "I understand you are troubled by how the elders of the tribes of Israel will receive you and that you do not speak well, which is why I am sending your older brother, Aaron, with you on this mission."

Aaron would be indispensible to the success of the undertaking. He was the first-born son of Amram and a Levite priest, which gave him standing. In the ancient Near East, it was believed the firstborn son had priority to represent the family, that is, after the father. Primogeniture, the state of being the firstborn son, carried with it a number of special privileges, such as the birthright, which was a double portion of the family estate and the right to inherit the estate after the death of the father. Thus, in any formal dealings with the elders, it would be Aaron who would be the front man.

The elders of Israel wouldn't have listened to Moses without his older brother leading the way. Aaron would appear before them attired in his resplendent priestly garments, whereas his younger brother would be wearing the drab clothing of a shepherd. The elders would look askance at him and would turn their attention immediately to his brother. With his facile tongue, Aaron would succeed in convincing them that Moses was indeed God's chosen instrument to lead the tribes out of bondage.

Moses was amenable to taking on the mission, but reassessing its prospects only led to increasing doubts about its outcome. He didn't understand why El Shaddai, who was now calling himself I AM, had brought up the name of Ikhnaten from out of the past. He had heard about the Aten cult in his youth, but it never appealed to him, and during his years in Egypt he continued to worship Amun-Ra as most Egyptians did.

The LORD God now continued: "Let me explain something about Ikhnaten. He only identified his god as the sun-god and didn't see beyond that." I AM paused before resuming. "I am more than a sun-god. I am the cause of the sun and the moon and all the stars in the heavens and everything under the sun and everything beyond the sun, because...I AM...GOD."

Now Moses got it! Now he understood what El Shaddai actually represented. How do we know he got it? He confirms it for us in his own words. Of the 150 psalms in the Bible, one, Psalm 90, is attributed to Moses. He wrote: "...from everlasting to everlasting *You are God*" [my italics].

Moses' world of the 13th century BCE was a polytheistic world. People had no inkling as yet as to how the natural world functioned, and for them there was no distinction between the natural world and what we understand to be the supernatural realm. They had gods for everything to explain natural phenomena and to be appealed to for everyday help. Even the Hebrews of the patriarchs' time and those in Goshen were not monotheists but henotheists/polytheists. Ikhnaten realized the gods didn't exist: there was only the Aten. Moses was now thinking along the same lines. Vanquish the gods as Ikhnaten had done and replace them with one all-powerful Creator, the God of everything, El Shaddai recast as the one and only God. Now Moses realized that this god, God, could actually effect the liberation of His people...with Moses assisting Him.

He didn't want to admit it, but earlier he really thought the proposed venture was sheer folly. How could he alone – well, he would be aided by a relatively minor god, El Shaddai – convince Pharaoh, who had a mighty army at his disposal, to let the Hebrew slaves go? And why would Pharaoh agree to lose the services of an enslaved workforce of five thousand able-bodied workmen even for one week,[65] who were building his new capital in the Nile Delta? Now Moses saw it all differently: his God indeed was almighty – and with this god, the re-envisioned El Shaddai who called Himself by his eternal name, I AM, the plan could work.

As a final encouragement, I AM added: "You, Moses, have something Ikhnaten didn't have – you have experienced Me." The ultimate human experience!

---

65   Exodus 3:18 – Moses' deceptive strategy was to ask Pharaoh for an outing of only one week: three days journey in the desert, one day for the tribes to worship their God, and three days back to Goshen. Did Pharaoh see through this simple scheme, which we would consider simple-minded? Before you say yes, remember you're in the 21st century and equipped with secondary-process thinking. Pharaoh was limited to primary-process thinking.

CHAPTER 12

Aaron navigated his way successfully through a sea of questions posed by the elders of Israel. Moses managed a few comments,[66] which didn't hurt his cause.

However, the brothers encountered resistance from their cousin, Pharaoh Ramesses ll, when they broached the subject of having him terminate the bondage of the Hebrew tribes: "Who is the LORD,[67] that I should obey his voice to let Israel go? I know not the LORD, neither will I let Israel go" (Ex. 5:2). The struggle was now between ultimate proxies: I AM pitted against Amun-Ra.

Moses only recently, at the burning bush, learned God's preferred name, I AM, or LORD (often written in English as "the LORD God"). Pharaoh would have heard the Hebrews call their god El Shaddai or Elohim, not LORD. It is also premature to refer to the 12 tribes as Israel, the unified people and nation Moses *will* create. Both uses would be considered anachronistic. What it adds up to is that the above text was written much later than the 13th century BCE, the actual time of the action.

With Pharaoh's refusal to let the Hebrew tribes go, God launched the first of what would be a series of plagues to convince Pharaoh to free the Hebrews: "Thus saith the LORD, In this thou shalt know that I am the LORD: behold, I will smite with the rod that is in mine hand upon the waters which are in the river, and

---

66   Twice, in Exodus 6:12 and 6:30, Moses says that he is "of uncircumcised lips," meaning he is unskilled at speaking, something we have already been made aware of.

67   LORD (in caps) is the English translation of the Hebrew YHVH and is the equivalent of I AM, which, remember, is an abbreviated version of I AM THAT I AM (*ehyeh asher ehyeh* in Hebrew).

they shall be turned to blood" (Ex. 7:17). In modern-day thinking, the waters of the Nile turned red due to a red tide, or algal bloom.

Red tides are not uncommon and are caused by dense accumulations of algae near the water's surface. There are thousands of species of algae, and some of these contain red pigment. Hence the name red tide. And there are harmful algal blooms called toxic red algae.

Once the Nile waters became contaminated with toxic red algae, the fish began to die. Decaying fish polluted the river still further, forcing the frogs to take to dry land in droves, which set up the second plague, and that would be followed by a number of other plagues in what would be considered Nature's own chain reaction.

The Egyptologist Flinders Petrie described the process succinctly in 1911: "The order of the plagues was the natural order of such troubles on a lesser scale in the Egypt season, as was pointed out long ago." Indeed, red tide, for instance, was known long ago in Egypt. *The Admonitions of Ipuwer*, an ancient text dated to about 1600 BCE, included the statement: "Lo, the Nile overflows yet none plow for it...Lo, the river is blood...."

With each plague, Pharaoh held his ground and would not let the people go. He spent hours on his knees praying before a colossal stone statue to his god: "O magnificent Amun-Ra, most powerful god amongst the gods, who defeated the Sherden sea pirates and overcame the Hittite's celestial lord Tarhunt at Kadesh, humble this menial deity the Hebrew slaves worship."

The plagues kept coming, and the tenth plague would prove too much even for Pharaoh, who saw himself as the greatest king among kings[68] and the mightiest among men. The firstborn of

---

68   Shelley wrote about Rameses II with his poem "Ozymandias," the
      Greek equivalent of his name: "My name is Ozymandias, King of

the Egyptians would die in the night the Hebrews would forever commemorate as the Passover.

Perhaps it was a virulent bacterial or viral agent that spread rapidly throughout the Nile Delta but spared Goshen – thanks to a favorable wind or immunity that the Hebrews had. Whatever it was, it caused the deaths of large numbers of firstborn sons, including the king's.[69] Other sons and daughters and parents and grandparents died as well. Given the special status firstborn sons enjoyed in ancient cultures, the writer of Exodus mentions only them (consistent with the parsimonious writing style at the time).

With the death of his own son, Pharaoh acknowledged the power of the god of the Hebrews over Amun-Ra. He ended the struggle and let the people go.

I AM had engineered the victory. Moses was His instrument, and Aaron spoke his brother's words that came from God.

For Moses, God alone ruled the world, and he, the second monotheist,[70] was His prophet. He and I AM now developed the most extraordinary dyadic relationship in history.

Kings;/Look on my Works ye Mighty and despair...."

69   Ramses II had between 48 and 50 sons and 40–53 daughters by two wives and a number of concubines. He was succeeded by his thirteenth son, Merenptah.

70   I go along with the consensus opinion that Ikhnaten was the first.

CHAPTER 13

Moses knew the way to the Mountain of God. He had traveled the ancient route between Egypt and Midian twice, once going and then returning, and the less traveled path from his home in Madiam to the sacred mountain annually for forty years. His skills as a military leader handling thousands of men enabled him to organize the 20,000 or so Hebrews for the journey to the Promised Land.

The Book of Numbers, the fourth book of the Torah (Pentateuch, Five Books of Moses), deals with numbers, all sorts of numbers, including how many Israelites departed Egypt with Moses. Numbers 1:45–6 notes that he had 603,550 men from 20 years of age and upward "able to go forth to war." When we add women, children, older men, and non-Israelites to the mix, the number of people trekking *their* way to Mount Sinai with *Moshe* (Moses) sometime during the 13th century BCE comes to over 2 million.

The modern academic study of the Bible, noted for challenging traditional belief, considers the notion of 2-million people wandering the Sinai desert quite implausible. As N.H. Snaith wrote in Peake's Commentary on the Bible, "When on the march, they would constitute a column twenty-two miles long, marching 50 abreast with one yard between each rank." It does strain credulity.

Marching, let's assume, 10 abreast, and not including their donkeys, herds of cattle, and flocks of sheep and goats, they would have formed a column 150 miles long, according to archeologist Eric H. Cline (*From Eden to Exodus*). Even more preposterous.

Moses assembled the tribes at Rameses near Goshen and they proceeded to their first campsite, Succoth, about 25 miles to the southeast. The text states that they were in a hurry: "And the Egyptians were urgent upon the people, that they might send them out of the land in haste…And the people took their dough before it was leavened…" (Exodus 12:33–4). The front end of the column reached Succoth by sundown, but the bulk of the people – using Cline's guidelines – would still be back in Rameses. That is not making haste.

When you think about it, if Moses had over six hundred thousand fighting men, the Israelites would have been able to fend off Pharaoh's pursuing forces at the Red Sea and would not have required the most celebrated miracle in the Hebrew Bible to save them. Recall, it took Ramesses a year to amass an army of 20,000 to attack the Hittites at Kadesh. By comparison, Moses' 600,000 men would have been a juggernaut and the largest army in the world.

Consider also, as the Israelites neared Mount Sinai, they were attacked by a nomadic tribe, the Amalekites. Exodus 17:8–13 describes the ensuing day-long battle, which went back and forth until the Israelites finally won out. The Amalekites had attacked with an army of perhaps several thousand and were met presumably by an equal numerical force of Israelites. If Moses' troops had indeed numbered some 600,000, it would have been a slaughter.

Concerning the battle, "And it came to pass, when Moses held up his hand, that Israel prevailed: and when he let down his hand Amalek prevailed" (Ex. 17:11). Finally, Aaron and Hur held up his arms, and the struggle ended in victory.

That's the author's storytelling version a thousand years after the Exodus. A more likely scenario: Moses, the old field general, was positioned on high ground above the battle signaling to Joshua and the troops below using hand signals; that is, he was communicating by a 13th-century BCE version of semaphore.

Another point, Deuteronomy 7:7 stresses that the LORD chose Israel even though "ye were the fewest of all people." According to

the *Encyclopedia of the Archeology of Ancient Egypt*, Egypt's population at the time was 3 million. With a Goshenite population of
2 million, two-thirds that of mighty Egypt, the Israelites would
hardly qualify as "the fewest of all people."

The three most important items needed to cross the Sinai
desert successfully, which is to say, to come out alive, were water,
water, water. Moses was traveling along what was already an
ancient caravan route, averaging about 25 miles a day. Some days
it might be 30 or 35 miles. It all depended on where the next
oasis was. There would never be enough water at a stop-over for
2-million people. For 20,000, yes.

Chapter 2 of Exodus only mentions two midwives, Shiphrah
and Puah, for a supposed Goshen census of 2 million, half of
whom we can define as female. No two-tandem team of midwives
could handle such a work load, but they could a population of
20,000. To their glory, they showed themselves to be resistant to
their king's edict to drown all newborn male Hebrews: "And the
midwives said unto Pharaoh, Because the Hebrew women are not
as the Egyptian women; for they are lively, and are delivered ere
the midwives come in unto them" (Ex. 1:19). In other words, the
Hebrew women would self-deliver without any fuss before the
midwives would arrive on the scene.

Even though the text clearly states there were only two midwives: "And the king of Egypt spake to the Hebrew midwives of
which the name of one was Shiphrah, and the name of the other
Puah" (Ex. 1:15), adherents to Goshen's mega-population theory
insist there were many more; Shiphrah and Puah, they explain,
were in charge of them. Here they find support from the medieval
poet, philosopher, biblical scholar, astronomer, and Hebrew gram-
marian Rabbi Abraham Ibn Ezra (1089–1164), who maintained
that the two midwives collected taxes from the other accouch-
euses. Brilliant as he was, for he was one of the sparkling gems of

the Golden Age of Spain, Ibn Ezra's erudition did not extent to 13th-century BCE accouchement practices in Goshen, Egypt.

In a 1998 issue of *Vetus Testamentum*, the scholars' journal on the Old Testament, British scientist Colin Humphreys, author of *The Miracles of Exodus*, came up with a reasonable re-interpretation of the number of fighting men under Moses' command.

For Humphreys, it all boiled down to a key Hebrew word, *'eleph*, translated as "a thousand" in the Numbers passage. But *'eleph* also carries the meaning of a "group," such as a tribe, clan, family, or troop, as in a troop of soldiers. Numbers 1:21 states, in English, that the number of fighting men in the tribe of Reuben was 46,500. In the Hebrew text, this is represented as 46 *'eleph* and 500 men, which is 46 thousand and 500 men. Humphreys suggests it should be read as 46 troops and 500 men. That is, the tribe of Reuben contributed 500 men from 46 troops, not 46,500.

A troop would have between 10 and 20 men, which was standard for armies at the time (supported by data contained in the 14th-century BCE Amarna tablets[71] from Egypt). All in all, Humphreys, employing a sophisticated mathematical analysis, calculated a total of 5500 men making up Moses' fighting force. And a more realistic estimate of the number of Israelites participating in the Exodus would be about 20,000, not the multitude recorded in scriptural translation but enough to have guaranteed the birth of a nation.

---

71   Clay tablets containing diplomatic correspondence between officials in Memphis and representatives in Canaan and what is now Lebanon. These were letters written in Akkadian cuneiform, the diplomatic language, dated to 1404–1340 BCE.

CHAPTER 14

Regardless of the actual route Moses and the Israelites followed, they were headed for Aqaba at the head of the Gulf of Aqaba. "…God led the people…through the way of the wilderness of the Red Sea…." (Ex. 13:18). But there is controversy over whether the text actually refers to the Red Sea or a "Sea of Reeds."

There's no problem reading the verse in English, which has *yam suph* translated as "Red Sea." The Hebrew *yam* refers to a sea, lake, or river, and raises no translational issue. But *suph* translates as reeds, rushes, marshes. Thus *yam suph* is quite rightly rendered as "Sea of Reeds," not "Red Sea."

Leading biblical scholars, such as the "three H's," James Hoffmeier, Cornelius Houtman, and James Philip Hyath, maintain that the Israelites waded through a marshy "sea of reeds." Most modern scholars have followed suit.

On the other hand, we have the Septuagint, the 3rd-century BCE Greek translation of the Hebrew Bible, which rendered *yam suph* as *eruthra thalassa*, Greek for "Red Sea." It should be noted that the translators, 72 Alexandrian Jewish scholars, didn't use the Greek words for "sea of reeds."

They understood only too well that *yam suph* literally meant "sea of reeds," but they also knew that *yam suph* actually was the Red Sea. The tradition from Moses to the time of the Septuagint held that *yam suph* was indeed the Red Sea, not the Reed Sea.

In 1 Kings 9:26, we read, "And King Solomon made a navy of ships in Ezion Geber, which is besides Eloth, on the shore of the Red Sea [*yam suph*], in the land of Edom." Solomon was building fighting ships to sail on a body of water and not through marshland.

A thousand years later, we have New Testament references to the Red Sea – in Acts 7:36: "[Moses] brought them out after he had shown wonders and signs in the land of Egypt, and in the Red Sea...." And Hebrews 11:29: "By faith they passed through the Red Sea...." – that use eruthra thalassa, the Greek for Red Sea.

In th 4th century CE translation of the Hebrew Bible, the Vulgate, St. Jerome rendered *yam suph* as *mare rubrum* to designate the Red Sea, and the King James Version of the Bible (1611) also translated *yam suph* as Red Sea. The translators knew exactly what they were doing.

Indeed, as already confirmed, *yam suph* means "sea of reeds," but all the biblical citations imply a Red Sea crossing, not a soggy march through an inland reedy lake, such as Lake Timsah or the Bitter Lakes, a day's journey from Rameses, Moses' starting point, and two of the modern scholars' favorite candidates for the "Sea of Reeds."

Moses began the Exodus from Rameses (modern Qantir) in the Nile Delta and followed one of the established trade routes to the head of the Gulf of Aqaba. If you saw the film *Lawrence of Arabia*, Aqaba will sound familiar.

But where are we geographically in this account? you may be asking. Well, hold up your left hand, the dorsum (back) facing away from you, and spread your forefinger and middle finger as far apart as you can. Your forefinger pointing northwest will be the Gulf of Suez, and your middle finger pointing northeast, the Gulf of Aqaba. Between the two fingers is the Sinai Peninsula. The meat of your hand represents the main body of the Red Sea.

The two gulfs are projections or extensions of the Red Sea and as such are parts of the Red Sea. In ancient times, the gulfs themselves would also be referred to as the Red Sea. As for Aqaba, it is at the head of the Gulf of Aqaba (the tip of your middle finger).

The Red Sea, like the Caribbean and North Seas, is a salty sea, as opposed to, for example, the Sea of Galilee, an inland freshwater lake. Reeds grow only in freshwater rivers, lakes, and seas, not in saltwater seas. The salty Gulf of Aqaba is reed-free, yet it is called *yam suph*, "sea of reeds." Since the Red Sea and its Gulf of Aqaba extension are salt-water bodies, why would Moses have expected to find fresh water, and plenty of it, at Aqaba?

Here is where I have to pause to say something about Colin J. Humphreys, mineral engineer, physicist, chemist, astronomer, geologist, and researcher in micro-printing, perpetual light bulbs, and computer chips in the brain, as well as amateur archeologist and lay biblical scholar, in brief, a contemporary polymath, and my chief source for an up-to-date analysis of the Book of Exodus.

Humphreys is in the vanguard of scholars who are bringing the disciplined methodology and innovative tools of modern science to the study of the Bible. When it comes to the Red Sea versus Reed Sea controversy, the case he presents in his book, *The Miracles of Exodus*, is quite compelling.

Accompanied by his wife, he spent the Easter week of 1999 at Taba, on the western shore of the Gulf of Aqaba, playing botanical detective. To shorten a long story, he did find great clumps of freshwater reeds, four to six feet high, growing at the northernmost part of the gulf. He also found evidence that in Roman times the gulf extended farther north than today's shore and was – and this is fascinating – a reservoir of considerable fresh water.

How did Humphreys come to find what no one else had ever found? The answer is surprisingly simple: no one had bothered to look. It is in their nature for scientists to bother to look.

CHAPTER 15

Moses was actually sparring with Pharaoh during the time of the ten plagues. What he was asking for was permission to take the Israelites out into the desert some 75 miles from Goshen to spend one day offering sacrifices to their God, and then they would return, having been gone for a period of 7 days. Only Moses had no intention of returning. He had secured sufficient provisions from the anguishing Egyptians to make it to the tip of the Gulf of Aqaba, where he would find fresh water and food to continue the journey to Madian in Midian – and then proceed on to the Mountain of God.

Of course, after the third day, Moses kept going. Pharaoh's spies, who had been shadowing the Israelites' movements, hied back to Rameses to inform Pharaoh as to what was transpiring. Without a moment's hesitation, the king called out the troops, and the pursuit was on. He trapped Moses a mile or so south of Aqaba, and here is where the LORD God pulled off His most spectacular miracle for the Israelites.

Exodus 14:21 reads: "And Moses stretched out his hand over the sea, and the LORD caused the sea to go back by a strong east wind all that night, and made the sea dry land…."

And that is the way it happened – if you make one allowance. The ancients recognized four points on the compass: north, south, east, and west. You don't find them identifying northeast, northwest, et cetera. If you accept the east wind mentioned above to be a northeast wind, then Exodus 14:21 works.

With only a smidgen of knowledge of oceanography and meteorology, you can understand modern science's explanation of the parting of the waters of the Red Sea. Moses and the Israelites are trapped up against the Gulf of Aqaba, which is an extension of the Red Sea and was referred to as the "Red Sea" (*yam suph*) in Moses' day, about a mile or two south of Aqaba.

A strong wind, probably a gale, blowing from the *northeast* (the Bible's east wind) along the length of the gulf forced the water line back, creating several miles of dry land. The process is not an unfamiliar one and is referred to as wind setdown.[72] It would last for several hours, enough time for the Israelites to cross the gulf into Midian. As the wind weakened, the water would come gushing back as a wave called a bore, something like a tsunami.

Wind setdown, also known as wind tide, isn't all that rare. A strong wind blowing along Lake Erie, where wind setdown occurs from time to time, has been recorded to have caused water elevation differences of 16 feet between Toledo and Buffalo. On February 17, 1998, wind tide at the same lake produced a water level difference of 5 feet between the two cities.

Strong northeast winds blowing down the Gulf of Aqaba are fairly common. Pharaoh did not drown when the bore wave engulfed his army. He and his generals would have been directing the action from high ground. In fact, with his understanding of local weather phenomena, Pharaoh would never have had his chariots pursue the fleeing Israelites across the gulf. The essence of the biblical account is probably true, but the rest is embellishment. If the time ever comes when the Saudi government permits western archeologists to explore the northernmost waters of the Gulf of Aqaba, they will most likely find only a few rusty bicycles, not dozens of barnacle-encrusted chariots.

---

72 "Wind setdown is the drop in water level caused by wind stress acting on the surface of a body of water for an extended period of time." (Quoted from oceanographers Carl Drews and Weiqing Han's online PLoS One article, "Dynamics of Wind Setdown at Suez and the Eastern Nile Delta," 2010.)

CHAPTER 16

In the Acts of Peter, one of the early apocryphal writings, Peter flees Rome and crucifixion. Along the road, he meets the risen Jesus and asks him: "*Quo vadis?*" (Where are you going?) Jesus replies: "I am going to Rome to be crucified again." Finding new courage, Peter returns to Rome to carry on with his ministry and is crucified upside-down.[73]

We can now ask the question of Moses: "Quo vadis?" I have him going east into the land of the Midianites, whereas the guardians of the faith, Jewish or Christian, have him headed deep down into the Sinai Peninsula. They could be right, of course, but I will stick with Midian.

The *qua via* confusion can be attributed, at least indirectly, to the Roman emperor Constantine, the man who made it possible for Christianity to become a world religion. Constantine became Constantine the Great when he defeated his arch rival, Maxentius, at Rome's Milvian Bridge in 312 CE. It wasn't only that Maxentius, who controlled Rome, had a powerful army, but Constantine saw him as a tyrant armed with "wicked magical enchantments." He would need more than a powerful army of his own to overcome his adversary: the situation called for divine assistance against Maxentius' forces *and his gods*. Constantine turned to the God of his father, Constantius Chlorus (*Caesar* from 293–306), who had pretented all his life to be a pagan but was a Christian. (Once

---

73   The account is also included in the novel *Quo Vadis*, written by Polish author Henryk Sienkiewicz, winner of the Nobel Prize in literature in 1905. MGM came out with a movie adaptation of the book in 1951, starring Robert Taylor and Peter Ustinov, which received international recognition.

again, the battle wasn't only – or primarily – between men but between their gods.)

The early Church historian and Bishop of Caesarea Eusebius Pamphili, in his *The Life of the Blessed Emperor Constantine*, described vividly what happened to Constantine before the battle. At about noon, he had a vision. He saw "the sign of a cross of light in the heavens" with the inscription: "By this symbol you will conquer." That night, in a dream, "the Christ of God appeared to him with the same sign he had seen in the heavens and commanded him to make a likeness of that sign...."

The chronicler Lucius Lactantius, who would became tutor to Constantine's sons and one of the emperor's chief advisors, gives us the rest of Constantine's mystical experience. In his dream, the voice of the Christian God directs him "to delineate the heavenly sign on the shields of his soldiers." He had his soldiers paint *Chi-Rho*, the first two letters of Christ's name in Greek, on their shields. The *Chi-Rho* symbol was an early christogram, a combination of letters that formed an abbreviation of the name "Jesus Christ." Diagrammatically, the *chi* and *rho* (XP) are superimposed on one another so that the vertical stroke of the *rho* intersects the middle of the *chi*. Constantine attributed his victory to divine intervention.

The emperor's life was full of dreams and visions, which played an important, one might say, vital role in his scheme of things. Tradition has it that in 330 CE, his mother, Empress Helena, in response to one of her son's visions, had the hermits in the southern Sinai mountains build a small church to the Holy Virgin at the site of (what was assumed to have been) Moses' burning bush.

It was the early days of monasticism in the Sinai desert, a movement started by Saint Anthony, the "Father of all Monks," as he was known. He was born in Lower Egypt in 251, and when he was 18, his wealthy parents died. He turned to Scripture and took

Matthew 19:21 literally: "...If thou wilt be perfect, go and sell that thou hast, and give to the poor, and thou shalt have treasure in heaven: and come and follow me." He then embarked on the ascetic life. Disciples followed him into the desert, and a community based on his example of asceticism grew around him. His fame spread and reached as far as the Emperor in the Great Palace of Constantinople, who wrote him, praising him and asking for his prayers.

Why monks of the 3rd century selected a particular granite peak in the Sinai to be Jebel Musa ("the mountain of Moses") has never been made clear. At 7500 feet above sea level, the mountain is the highest in the area and, in sunlight or in fog, an awe-inspiring sight. The monks created Jebel Musa, and St. Helena's imprint guaranteed its prolonged shelf life. But more and more scholars are questioning Jebel Musa as the real Mountain of Moses. Nowadays it is considered only a "possible" location, one of a baker's dozen, of the biblical Mount Sinai.

In the 6th century, the Byzantine emperor Justinian (reigned 527–565) had a new magnificent church, St. Catherine's Monastery, built on the site of the ruins of St. Helena's original church. It was named for Catherine of Alexandria, condemned to death on the spiked wheel, which broke when she touched it. She was then beheaded, and tradition has it that angels took her remains to Mount Sinai. St. Catherine's Monastery became a magnet for Christian pilgrims beginning in the 6th century and continued to attract pilgrims and tourists right up to this day.

In brief, there is no archeological evidence to support the age-old assumption that Mount Sinai is in the south central Sinai Peninsula. A systematic investigation of the Sinai Peninsula only began after Israel had gained control of the peninsula in the 1967

Six-Day War.[74] The conclusion of a number of Israeli scholars, as stated by Itzhaq Beit-Arieh read: "Nowhere in Sinai did we... find any concrete remains of the stations on the Exodus route, nor even small encampments that could be attributed to the relevant period. Neither did we discover anything that would help us identify the Mountain of God..."(*Biblical Archeology Review* article, July-Aug. 1984).

We would do better to look to the Bible for our clues as to its location. Exodus 3:1 is staring us straight in the face: "Now Moses kept the flock of Jethro his father in law, the priest of Midian: and he led the flock to the *backside* [my italics] of the desert, and came to the mountain of God, even to Horeb."

The Hebrew for "backside" is *achar*, which is how the KJV translates it, whereas other translations go with "far side" and "west side." The backside would be the far side, that is, the eastern region of the Sinai desert as one approaches the Gulf of Aqaba starting from Rameses in the Nile Delta to the west. Moses and the Israelites were headed toward Midian, east of the far side of the Sinai desert.

---

74   Between 1967 and 1982, the Sinai was under Israeli control, when it was then returned to Egypt as part of the Israel-Egypt Peace Treaty of 1979.

CHAPTER 17

The Bible lets us know that Moses was going in the right direction. "And the LORD went before them by day in a pillar of a cloud, to lead them the way; and by night in a pillar of fire, to give them light; to go by day and night: He took not away the pillar of the cloud by day, nor the pillar of fire by night, from before the people" (Exodus 13:21–22).

Not that he needed to be shown the way to the Mountain of God, for Moses had traversed the route before, but it was reassuring to know the LORD was with him on his unparalleled migratory trek. The pillar of fire at night, a glowing night light in the Egyptian desert blackness, was another godsend; and with these signs from heaven, he knew the Almighty One, I AM as He now called Himself, would not fail him when the going hit rough spots, as he knew it would.

If with Exodus 13:21–22 you didn't catch where God was guiding Moses, then Exodus 19:16–19 should make it clear: "And it came to pass...that there were thunders and lightnings, and a thick cloud upon the mount, and the voice of the trumpet exceedingly loud...And mount Sinai was altogether on a smoke, because the LORD descended upon it in fire: and the smoke thereof ascended as the smoke of a furnace, and the whole mount quaked greatly. And when the voice of the trumpet sounded long, and waxed louder and louder, Moses spake...."And add Deuteronomy 4:11 to Exodus 13:21–22: "And ye came near and stood under the mountain; and the mountain burned with fire unto the midst of heaven, with [black] clouds, and thick darkness."

The holy mountain God is leading Moses to is a volcano – and it is an active volcano (or was active in the time of Moses).

These descriptions of Mt. Sinai bring to mind the letter Pliny the Younger wrote to the Roman historian Tacitus in 104 CE about the eruption of Mount Vesuvius, which he had witnessed in 79 CE: "There had been for several days before some shocks of earthquake, but that night they became so violent that one might think that the world was…turned topsy-turvy…[Issuing from their mouth of Vesuvius was] a black and dreadful cloud bursting out in gusts of igneous serpentine vapor now and again split open to reveal long fantastic flames, resembling flashes of lightning but much larger…Soon afterwards the clouds I have described began to descend to the sea…."

Fire and clouds of smoke are part and parcel of any erupting volcano, but the thunder and lightning or loud trumpet blasts require explanation. The lightning is due to static electricity acting on ash particles. As for the trumpet sounds, magma, which is molten volcanic rock, contains water vapor and carbon dioxide, and when these gases are forced out through cracks in the floor and surrounding area of the volcano, the noise they produce sounds like a trumpet blast.

It's interesting that volcanoes with a history of eruptions acquire the label of "mountain of God." For the Maasai of Tanzania, *Ol Doinyo Lengai* means "Mountain of God" in their language, Maa. *Ol Doinyo Lengai*, which is close to Mount Kilimanjaro (made famous by Hemingway with his 1936 short story, "The Snows of Kilimanjaro"), has erupted more than a dozen times in the past hundred years.

Pele, the Hawaiian goddess of fire, dwells inside Kilauea, the active volcano on the Big Island, and in the past was believed to be responsible for the volcano's eruptions. According to legend, it was the heated arguments between her and her sister Namakaokahai that led to the formation of the Hawaiian islands.

Mount Bromo, in East Java, Indonesia, is an active volcano. Its name, Bromo, is Javanese for Brahma, the Hindu creator god. For some of the indigenous peoples living in the Kamchatka Peninsula of Russia, the active volcano Klyuchevskaya Sopka is the spot where the world was created and is considered sacred.

There's a small volcano, *El Cerro de la Estrella* (the Hill of the Star), in the Mexico City neighborhood of Iztapalapa that was sacred to the Aztecs. Poet Octavio Paz called it the spot where the world was created. In the distance can be seen the volcanoes Popocateptl (last erupted in 1994) and Iztaccihuatl (dormant), also sacred mountains to the Aztecs.

Likewise, there is something special, in the arcane sense, about the mountain to which Moses is leading the Israelites. His father-in-law, Jethro, had introduced him to the mountain, which is where the Midianite priest's tribe worshipped their god. Now Moses' god, I AM, wants the Israelites to worship Him at the mountain of Jethro's god.

At this juncture, we do not know the name of Jethro's god. In Cecil B. DeMille's film *The Ten Commandments*, Moses' Midianite wife Zipporah refers to him as "He Who Has No Name," and the inference is that he and I AM are one and the same. This is not the case.

The DeMille motion picture does get the location of the holy mountain correct. Moses is in Jethro's bailiwick, Midian, and Ziporrah explains to him, "The mountain rumbles when God is there." Mt. Sinai is volcanic, and it *is* in Midian. *There are no volcanoes in the Sinai Peninsula.*

To the best of my knowledge, thirteen sites have been proposed for Mt. Sinai, and these are described in Menasche Har-el's *The Sinai Journeys: The Route of the Exodus*. Several authors, including Glen A Fritz (*Mountain on Fire*) and Howard Blum (*The Gold of Exodus: The Discovery of the True Mount Sinai*), claim that Jabal al-Lawz,[75] located in northwest Saudi Arabia, is the biblical Mt. Sinai.

---

75   The actual mountain thought to be Mt. Sinai is Jabal al-Maqla, which lies within the Jabal al-Lawz mountain range.

CHAPTER 18

The Book of Exodus never quite identifies Mount Sinai as being in Midian. Exodus 3:1 states that Moses…"led the flock to the backside of the desert [which would be in Midian], and came to the mountain of God." In Exodus 18:5, we still don't read "Midian" anywhere in the text, but we're getting closer: "And Jethro…came…unto Moses into the wilderness [in Midian], where he encamped at the mount of God."

Exodus 19:2 is intriguing: "For they were departed from Rephidim, and were come to the desert of Sinai, and had pitched in the wilderness; and there Israel camped before the mount." At Rephidim, the Israelites would encounter the Amalekites. I have already described the Battle of Rephidim, and soon I will state why the event helps us place Rephidim in Midian.

There is another clue that helps us place Mount Sinai in Midian. Deuteronomy 1:2 (NIV) reads: "It takes eleven days to go from Horeb to Kadesh Barnea by the Mount Seir road." Kadesh Barnea, the desert oasis where Moses and the Israelites spent thirty-eight years, is about forty-five miles south-southeast of Beersheba.

Mount Seir, according to *Smith's Bible Dictionary*, is the mountain ridge that lies between the *Wady Aly* and the *Wady Ghurab*. That's not much help. Genesis 32:3 reads: "And Jacob sent messengers before him to Esau his brother unto the land of Seir, the country of Edom," which God gave to Esau and his descendants, the Edomites. Not much help there either. In the literature, we find Edom even being referred to as Mount Seir, but my immediate task is to locate the Mount Seir road.

Mount Seir, to be brief, lies east of the Arabah, the geographic tract extending over the length of the Jordan Rift Valley, 8 to 13 miles wide, from the Sea of Galilee to the Dead Sea and on down to the tip of the Gulf of Aqaba. Just visualize dropping a plumb line from the southern tip of the Sea of Galilee all the way south to the tip of the Gulf of Aqaba, and that's the area being described.

Mount Seir is in today's Jordan, less than thirty miles from Petra, the ancient Nabataean capital. If it were west of the Arabah, Mt. Seir would be in the Sinai Peninsula, as would Mt. Sinai. But it is east of the Arabah, and the Mount Seir road runs over it or courses close to it.

With what's contained in Deuteronomy 1:2 plus a little help from volcanology, we can zero in on the actual location of Mount Sinai. To begin with, the Bible tells us it took 11 days to go, that is, walk from Horeb, the other name for Mt. Sinai, to Kadesh Barnea. A caravan in Moses' time traveling at a rate of 3 miles per hour would cover 24 miles in 8 hours, considered a day's travel, which would be 264 miles in 11 days. Of course, watering holes weren't stationed every 24 miles; so a caravan would keep going until it would come to the next oasis before calling it a day. Alois Musil, in *The Northern Hegaz*, writes that during the Middle Ages, pilgrims making the *Hajj* from Egypt to Mecca averaged 28–31 miles a day. Thus, the travelers would have covered 324 miles in eleven days (the average of 308 and 341). Pilgrims traveling from Damascus to Mecca did better, averaging 37.5 miles a day. In eleven days, they would have covered a distance of 412 miles. We can consider 412 miles to be the maximum distance from Kadesh Barnea to Horeb. If you draw an arc with a radius of 412 miles centered on Kadesh Barnea, then Horeb (Mount Sinai) lies within the arc.

We need a little help from volcanology. *Volcanoes of the World*, a compilation by prominent volcanologists, cites all the volcanoes that have been active these past 10,000 years: a total of 1511. Of the 1511, 18 are in Arabia, and only 3 lie within our arc. We are getting close to locating Mount Sinai.

East of the area of granite mountains called the Shifa lies the Hisma. Archeologist David Hogarth, in his *Handbook of Hejaz* (1917), called the Hisma "the hinterland" of Midian. The 3 volcanoes lying within the arc we drew are in the Midian hinterland.[76]

The salient geographic feature of the Hisma is a lava field extending about 135 miles in length, which can be divided into northern and southern halves, with a hollowed out area on the western side in the middle of the range. The northern lava field, called Harrat Rahah, contains an unnamed volcano, one of the three that could be Mt. Sinai.

Volcanoes of the World provides no information about the volcano in the Harrat Rahah. Fortunately, volume 16 of the 22-volume *Catalog of Active Volcanoes of the World* does and describes the volcano as a tuff cone, that is, a small volcanic cone, situated on a lava bed.

A volcano's eruptive capacity is rated on a scale called the VEI (volcanic explosivity index). A VEI of 0 indicates a nonexplosive eruption with a cloud column, referred to as a plume (mixture of particles and gases), of less than 300 feet. The unnamed volcano in the Harrat Rahah fits this description.

A gentle eruption with a plume rising as high as half a mile is given a VEI rating of 1. The 2011 Nabro eruption in the Red Sea off the coast of Eritrea produced an ash cloud of 8.7 miles, warranting a VEI of 3.

The 1883 Krakatoa eruption in the Dutch East Indies (Indonesia after 1949), with a VEI of 6, had an explosive force of 200 megatons of TNT and was heard 3000 miles away. The

---

76   The Midian region (NW Arabia) is bordered on the west by the Gulf of Aqaba and on the east by the Hisma.

eruption cooled the world's oceans, suppressing ocean level rises for decades.

Tambora, on Sumbawa island, Indonesia, erupted in 1815 leaving in its wake 88,000–92,000 deaths. Its plume reached 30 miles into the stratosphere. It has a Newhall-Self rating of 7. (The VEI was developed by volcanologists Christopher Newhall and Stephen Self in 1982.)

The highest VEI rating is 8, but there haven't been any Holocene (the present *epoch* beginning 11,650 years ago) eruptions with a VEI of 8. The most recent such super eruption, Lake Taupo's Oruanui in New Zealand, occurred about 26,500 years ago.

I have saved an explanation of a VEI of 2 for the last. These volcanic eruptions are explosive and produce plumes as high as 3 miles. However, a VEI of 2 will also be assigned to eruptions that are explosive but nothing else – plume, frequency of eruption, tropospheric/stratospheric[77] penetration – is known about them.

The volcano in the Harrat Rahah can be crossed off our list. It now all boils down to the other two volcanoes, which are located in the southern lava field called Harrat 'Uwayrid. These are named Hala-'l-'Ishqua and Hala-'l-Bedr.

Arabic writings mention a volcanic eruption in the Harrah area in 640 CE, which volcanologists attribute to either Hala-'l-'Ishqua or Hala-'l-Bedr. In *Volcanoes of the World*, 'Ishqua is given a VEI of 0, which means its eruption was nonexplosive with a plume no higher than 300 feet. Such an eruption would be visible for only a short distance. The volcanic eruption that guided the Israelites – "And the LORD went before them by day in a pillar of a cloud…

---

77   The troposphere, the lowest and densest part of the earth's atmosphere, extends from the earth's surface to the tropopause, the interface between the troposphere and the stratosphere, which begins at a height of about 7 miles.

and by night in a pillar of fire…" (Ex. 13:21) – could be seen for two hundred miles.

The last of the three Arabian volcanoes within eleven days' journey from Horeb (Sinai) to Kadesh Barnea and known to be historically active is Hala-'l-Bedr. *Volcanoes of the World* assigns Bedr a VEI of 2, that is, Bedr was considered an explosive volcano, with a plume of up to 3 miles.

The wording in *Volcanoes of the World* is clear: "Eruptions that were definitely explosive, but carry no other descriptive information in their record, have been assigned a default VEI of 2." Mount Bedr's VEI of 2 could actually be higher because, for all we know, its plume could have reached a height greater than 3 miles during an eruption.

Starting with 1,511 volcanoes, we have narrowed down our Mount Sinai choices to three and finally one. Of course, nothing in this life is certain except death and taxes, but it looks like the real Mt. Sinai is out there under the name of Mount Bedr.

CHAPTER 19

Mount Bedr presents an imposing sight. It is situated between Harrat Rahah and Harrat 'Uwayrid in the hollow mentioned above, which is a fertile, pale-green basin. Bedr sits by itself on a flat, grayish sandstone mountain table 5,000 feet above sea level, about six miles in diameter. The volcano, Bedr/Sinai, is a black, basaltic cone rising 500 feet above the table mountain, "like the huge altar of some natural temple," to borrow a simile biblical scholar Dean Stanley applied to Ras Safsafa, a towering peak in the same range as Jebel Musa in the Sinai Peninsula (and his choice for Mount Sinai).

Moses and the Israelites arrived at Bedr/Sinai 3 months after leaving Goshen: "In the third month, when the children of Israel were gone forth out of the land of Egypt, the same day came they into the wilderness of Sinai…and there Israel camped before the mount" (Ex. 19:1–2).

I have not dwelt on the route Moses followed from Rameses to Mt. Sinai. For the reader interested in knowing details about the stop-overs along the way, I recommend Colin Humphreys excellent book, *The Miracles of Exodus*.

It was at Rephidim that the Amalekites attacked the Israelites: "Remember what Amalek did unto thee by the way, when ye were come forth out of Egypt; How he…smote the hindmost of thee, even all that were feeble behind thee, and thou wast faint and weary; and he feared not God" (Deut. 25:17–18).

According to this biblical passage, the Amalekites knew about the Israelites' harrowing escape from Ramesses ll at the Gulf of Aqaba and initially attacked stragglers, easy pickings, for their Egyptian gold and silver, before finding themselves in a pitched battle with Moses' forces.

Earlier the Israelites berate Moses because there is no water. God solves the problem: "Behold, I will stand before thee there upon the rock in Horeb; and thou [Moses] shalt smite the rock, and there shall be water ouf of it…" (Ex. 17:6).

"Then came Amalek, and fought with Israel in Rephidim" (Ex. 17:8). But why are they fighting? Are the Amalekites only after loot? First of all, we have to locate Rephidim: it is in Horeb's back yard. Then we read how Moses smites the rock, the rock at Horeb, for water. The "rock at Horeb," is a metaphor for the porous sandstone table mountain on which Mt. Horeb (Mt. Sinai) sits.

Restated, the "rock at Horeb" refers to a *very* large porous "rock," that is, a sandstone or limestone mountain that can hold a great deal of water.

I cannot overemphasize the importance of water in sustaining life in the desert. Vera Nazarian, in her own way, confirms my point with this line from her *Dreams of the Compass Rose*: "In the desert, the only god is a well."[78] The Battle of Rephidim is more than a fight over water rights. Mount Bedr is the Amalekites' sacred mountain. It is where their god makes his home, and thus the Amalekites are protecting their holy turf. In losing the battle, they have lost their "mountain of God." Why the LORD God should want this pagan mountain for His people is a question that remains unanswered.

The defeat of the Amalekites, *and their god*, in the shadow of Mount Bedr was another illustration or demonstration of *El Shaddai*'s growing power and strength in the minds of the Israelites, who would come to know their deity as I AM only later when Moses descended from Mount Sinai with the two tablets of the Ten Commandments (Exodus 34:29). This would be another early step in a developmental process that would take centuries until the religion we know as Judaism finally emerged.

Moses didn't have to continue banging away at the porous mountain wall to supply the Israelites with water. The table mountain that housed Mt. Bedr on its eastern slope also had a spring flowing down its western slope, as Musil recorded in *The Northern Hegaz*.

The fertile green basin mentioned above, known as al-Gaw, "the watering place," contained an abundance of rainwater wells

---

78 Antoine de Saint-Exupery provides us with a sanguine view of the desert in his *The Little Prince*: "What makes the desert beautiful is that somewhere it hides a well."

and a variety of edible plants. Exodus 19:14 notes that the people washed their clothes, meaning there was plenty of water for the 20,000 Israelites, who were to spend eleven months at the holy mountain – and for the 40,000 Beli, a Bedouin tribe, who wintered in the al-Gaw plain when the intrepid Musil was there in 1910.

"The time has come," the Walrus said, "to talk of many things," wrote Lewis Carroll in his poem "The Walrus and the Carpenter." I have already talked about many things, but one thing remains unspoken: the meaning behind the names of many things talked about. For instance, the meaning of the name Sinai.

The word has two component parts, "sin" plus an ending, "ai." In moral theology, to sin means to deviate from God's law. But we're in the ancient Mideast where Sin was the name of a god: "The name Sin…almost certainly derived from the Babylonian Moon-god, Sin," wrote Alfred Lucas in his *The Route of the Exodus of the Israelites from Egypt* (1938).

Haran (or Harran) in Upper Mesopotamia and Ur in the region of Sumer, where Abraham (c. 2000 BCE or earlier) had lived, were cultic centers of Moon-god worship. The Moon-god was also worshipped at Tayma[79] in Midian dating back to the Bronze Age period, and temples in southern Arabia (now Yemen) have been uncovered by archeologists dedicated to the Moon-god.

The worship of the Moon-god was widespread throughout the Fertile Crescent (crescent-shaped land area from the eastern Mediterranean to the Persian Gulf). Interestingly, the Spanish for Fertile Crescent is *la media luna fertil* ("the fertile half moon").

The al-Hamra cube, discovered in the al-Hamra Temple in Tayma, is something worth mentioning. Dated to the 6th century BCE, the cube's length is fifteen inches. Humphreys, in *The Miracles of Exodus*, describes it thusly: "On one face of the cube are the

---

79   About 250 miles north of Medina.

crescent moon and a bull's head with crescent horns, both known to represent the Moon-god." Between the bull's horns is a disc, probably a representation of a full moon. The bull as a symbol – a young bull, it should be noted – is associated with moon worship. The relevancy of this paragraph about the al-Hamra cube will soon become evident.

Moon-god worship was spread out over a vast area, where a multitude of languages was spoken. In Babylonian, the god's name was Sin; in Sumerian, Nanna; Yarih in Ugaritic; Khonsu in Egyptian; et cetera. In Midian, it was Sin, although archeologists have not been able to determine who named the mountain Sinai. Jethro, the priest of Midian, served the Moon-god, Sin. We can assume that Moses, living under his father-in-law's roof for forty years and married to his daughter Zipporah, was a Moon-god worshipper during those two score years, just as he had worshipped another pagan god, Ammon, as his primary god earlier during his years as Prince Moses in Egypt.[80]

Bedr in Arabic means "full moon," and Mount Bedr is the "mountain of the full moon," which is the mountain of the Moon-god. The "ai" ending in Sinai means "belonging to," and Mount Sinai is the mountain of the Moon-god Sin.

The Israelites, under Moses' direction, displaced the Amalekites from the mountain home of their Moon-god and enthroned their own god in his place. However, not everyone was pleased with the idea of a pagan mountain as the abode for El Shaddai. Old ways die hard, and Moses' referring to their god as I AM was both baffling and disconcerting to a number of Israelites. In addition, their ancestral god, El Shaddai, was peripatetic. Why should He now

---

80　He may have worshipped Khonsu, the god of the moon, during his years living in Pharaoh's palace in Memphis.

be imprisoned in a mountain? Or as we in the 21st century might say, stuffed into a bottle like a genie.

There were enough discontented Israelites on this issue to be considered a significant minority, who could challenge Moses on his selection of Mt. Sinai as their holy site. The memory of the golden calf incident, with Moses hurtling death and destruction upon a rebellious throng, was still fresh in everyone's memory. No one wanted a repeat, and a compromise was reached. The dissidents would accept Moses' mountain, but they would not call it by the pagan name of Sinai. Instead, they gave it an Egyptian or possibly Proto-Arabic name that later, when Hebrew became their language, would be Horeb, which means "bleak," an apt description for the isolated, black mountain cone situated on the Tedra, the basalt table mountain that reached into the sky far above the lush al-Gaw valley.[81]

"You mean the Israelites, who were the Hebrews, didn't speak Hebrew in Moses' time?" was a typical interruption in my lecture I usually faced at this point.

Let me try to explain what's going on here. When in Egypt, the first forty years of his life, Moses spoke Egyptian. For the next forty years in Midian, he spoke what is generally labeled Proto-Arabic. Now, Midian was named for Midian,[82] one of the six sons Abraham had with his second wife Keturah after the death of Sarah (Exodus 25:1). Abraham spoke Cushitic Akkadian in his native Ur and possibly one or two of the many Nilo-Saharan languages. When he moved to Canaan, he acquired Early

---

81 The Sinai-Moon-god connection is presented in Colin Humphreys' *The Miracles of Exodus.*

82 Midian had five sons, Ephah, Epher, Hanoch, Abidah, and Eldaah, considered the progenitors of the Midianites.

Proto-Arabic. Moses in Midian, half a dozen or more centuries later, spoke Late Proto-Arabic.

Imagine this scene. The Exodus is underway, and Moses and his 20,000 have escaped the clutches of Pharaoh at the Red Sea. The Israelites have made it into Midian on their way to the Mountain of God, and Moses can afford to slow the pace. During a moment of relaxation, Joshua asks Moses just what was it he heard at the burning bush. The conversation is in Egyptian. Joshua and the Israelites have just come out of Egypt, where the 12 tribes have been speaking Egyptian for more than 400 years. Moses has to translate what he heard in Proto-Arabic into Egyptian. Once you start translating what you get is never quite the same as the original. An old Tuscan proverb says it well: *Traduttore traditore* ("Translators are traitors.")

Moses will die forty years after the Exodus (c. 1210 BCE, with the Exodus dated to 1250). Before his death, near the end of the 13th century BCE, the Israelites begin to come into contact with what is a new language. A number of languages have recently developed out of Proto-Canaanite: Moabite, Phoenician, Edomite, *Hebrew*, Ugaritic, et cetera. The Israelites are only too happy to rid themselves of Egyptian, for them the language of slavery, and they take to Hebrew. I know it sounds odd that only now the Hebrews begin to speak Hebrew. There is a case for identifying the Hebrews as one of the groups in the Fertile Crescent known as *habiru*, tent wanderers, who date back to the early centuries of the 2nd millennium BCE; so the matter is a little more complicated than the way I present it.

Now what Moses heard at the burning bush in Proto-Arabic, initially translated into Egyptian, is re-translated into Early Hebrew. By the 6th century BCE, during the Babylonian Exile, when scribes have begun writing what will become the Holy Bible, the I AM identification passage – what we read as Exodus

3:14 – appears for the first time in Biblical Hebrew. More than a thousand years will have passed from Moses' century until we have the definitive canon. All that is left to us over this span of time of what God was explaining about Himself to Moses in 3:14 – an extensive dialogue between God and Moses still floating somewhere in the ether but lost to us – is *ehyeh asher ehyeh* – I AM THAT I AM.

What were the actual words God said to Moses in Proto-Arabic at the burning bush? It was probably something close to I AM THAT I AM. Perhaps I AM HE WHO MADE YESTERDAY, WHO MADE TODAY, AND WHO WILL MAKE TOMORROW. The Hebrew, *ehyeh asher ehyeh*, is close enough – whatever the original wording in Proto-Arabic may have been – to how God wanted Himself known to us. In whatever the language, God is saying He is self-existent and exists outside of time and space.

When all is said and done, we, in Judaism, are left with one sacred name for God, the Tetragrammaton, YHVH,[83] Yahveh,[84] a representation of *ehyeh asher ehyeh*, I AM THAT I AM. God had convinced Moses at the burning bush that He was more than El Shaddai, a tribal god – He was God. Moses' task now was to teach his people what he understood about God, and the teaching would begin at the holy mountain, Mount Sinai.

He was starting from scratch, with a people who were at the polytheistic-henotheistic level of spiritual development. Once safe from Pharaoh and his pursuing army, the Israelites paused on the eastern shore of the Red Sea to give thanks to their god, El Shaddai, for their deliverance, expressed in a poem, the "Song of the Sea" (Exodus 15: 1–18): Miriam sings out: "Who among the

---

83   YHWH is derived from the Hebrew root *hwy*, meaning "to be."

84   Jehovah for Christians.

gods is like unto thee, O LORD?" She is referring to El Shaddai, not her brother Moses' I AM.

"LORD" spelled in caps, signifying Yahveh, is incorrect in this instance. There is no indication in the text that Moses thus far has shared his awareness of God as the I AM with the Israelites, including Aaron and Miriam. At this stage, he is alone as a monotheist.

In DeMille's *The Ten Commandments*, Ramesses returns to his palace after his failure at the Red Sea. Nefertari, his wife, who loves/hates Moses,[85] says to him: "Where is his blood on your sword?" (In other words, she wanted him dead.) Ramesses, having now recognized who Moses' god is, drops his sword and in dismay utters what is the most enduring line in the film: *"His god is God."* Does this mean that Ramesses, too, has become a member of the monotheist club? As Alfred Hitchcock calmly reminded one of his actors who apologized excessively for flubbing his lines during a filming: "It's only a movie."

There remains the intriguing episode of the Golden Calf. Here's the setting. Moses has ascended to the holy mountain's peak, where he awaits word from God, his I AM. The 20,000 below on the Tadra have been growing steadily anxious with each passing day without the re-appearance of their leader. To make matters worse, the mountain, which is a volcano, begins to rumble and spit fire and smoke. The Israelites are from Egypt, where there are no volcanoes, and they are frightened out of their wits. Finally, after forty days and nights, panic sets in.

They have only been in Midian a short while but have already learned who's who among the Midianite gods. For them, all is lost

---

85 Good portrayal in the film of what Freud meant by ambivalence. She loves Moses, but he has spurned her: "Hell hath no fury like a woman scorned" (from playwright William Congreve's *The Mourning Bride*.

without their leader Moses, who they believe has been devoured by the god of the mountain, the Moon-god.

In their panic, they pressure Aaron, the priest of Israel, who dubs as a goldsmith, to make them a golden calf to placate the angry god of the mountain. He fashions a young bull, actually a calf, with crescent-shaped horns – the symbol of the Moon-god.

"And they rose up early on the morrow, and offered burnt offerings…"(Ex. 32:6). In DeMille's biblical epic, Lilia, Joshua's love interest, is about to be offered up as a burnt sacrifice by Dathan, one of the leaders in opposition to Moses's authority, when Moses appears out of the mist with the Ten Commandments. He takes care of the chieftains and brings an end to the profane revelry of their followers.

The account is not an illustration of the familiar saying, When the cat's away, the mice will play, nor is it necessarily a tale of apostasy, the way it is usually interpreted. The people were led astray because of what they perceived to be the imminent threat of death. Since the golden calf failed to protect them and they were about to die, they might as well go out with a memorable orgy. It would be the opposite of T.S. Eliot's "The Hollow Men" ending: "This is the way the world ends/Not with a bang but a whimper."

We still read about Moon-god worship in the Bible more than three hundred years after the Exodus: "Whereupon the king [Jeroboam] took counsel, and made two calves of gold, and said unto them, It is too much for you to go up to Jerusalem: behold thy gods, O Israel, which brought thee up out of the land of Egypt"(1 Kings 12:28).

Biblical chronologist Edwin R. Thiele dates Jeroboam's reign from 931 to 910 BCE. He made Shechem the capital of the Northern Kingdom and, what interests us here, built two state temples housing ornate golden calves, one in Dan in the north of Israel (Northern Kingdom) and the other in Bethel at its southern border. The bull-calf idol in the Bethel temple survived as an object of worship until the late 7th century BCE, when King Josiah (c. 649–606 BCE) had it demolished. Josiah, who died in his late thirties, is well summarized in 2 Kings 22:2: "And he did that which was right in the sight of the LORD, and walked in all the way of David his father, and turned not aside to the right hand or to the left." But it would not be accurate to say that he succeeded in abolishing idolatry during his reign, which was a fixture throughout the ancient world.

Interestingly, the only source of Josiah's existence that we have is the biblical account. No archeological evidence or surviving texts from Egypt or Babylon or anywhere else in the ancient Mideast has ever been found. Very few documents about him of any kind, such as inscriptions, have come down to us from that time period. Not surprisingly, I couldn't find what happened to the other golden calf, the one in the temple in Dan. (Perhaps I should mention that the most famous resident of Dan was the judge Samson; in Hebrew, Dan means "judge," and for the record, Daniel, which is *Dan + el*, means "God is my judge.")

The story of the Golden Calf is told in chapter 32, and for those who will read it in English, it should be read in the King James translation. The KJV simulates the simplicity of language as spoken in the 13th century BCE. The English Standard Version (ESV), just to consider one of the various modern translations, is clearer, of course, easier for today's reader, but it fails to capture the level of mental functioning of the people, as reflected in language, in the distant time of Moses. I would like to be able to read the accounts of the Golden Calf and Moses at the burning bush in Proto-Arabic, that archaic tongue only the angels remember.

However, they are available in Coptic, the liturgical language of the Coptic Orthodox Church, the sole surviving form of ancient Egyptian. Joseph and his descendants in Egypt spoke Middle

Egyptian (2000–1300 BCE). The Israelites of Moses' time spoke Late Egyptian (1300–700 BCE).

God parting the waters of the Red Sea stands out as His greatest miracle in all the biblical stories, but as you have read, the miracle can be explained in terms of natural phenomena. If there is nothing supernatural about it, then it is not a miracle. Nevertheless, it is just that: a miracle. The miracle is in how God structured events so that Moses and the Israelites would be where they had to be at the right moment for the waters of the Red Sea to part for them. If they were pinned up against the Gulf of Aqaba just a few miles farther south and if they had been a day earlier or a day later, there would have been no crossing, that is, no miracle.

Psalm 77:14 summarizes God's power with one line: "You are the God who performs miracles." Of course, this holds true for those who believe that God is transcendent, which means He is beyond time and space, and yet immanent, that is, involved here on earth. Reworded, this is God's universe and God is in charge – for those who believe in salvation history.

CHAPTER 20

Earlier, Pharaoh Ikhnaten was described as the first modern man, and Moses was seemingly patterned after him. The comparison to Ikhnaten works but only to a degree. Consider the account in Numbers 21:4–9, where Moses' remedy for snakebite is to have those bitten gaze upon a bronze serpent on a pole and be healed. This example of faith healing would have been dismissed out of hand by the rational-minded Ikhnaten.

Can Moses, said to be a monotheist like Ikhnaten, be considered the second modern man? If so, then why is he portrayed in the Book of Exodus as an archaic man? We see that his faith in YHVH has fortified him and imbued him with absolute confidence for the task of shepherding 20,000 Israelites across hundreds of miles of no-man's- land to a distant holy mountain. Yet, he displays so many of the characteristics of a man who appears not to have progressed beyond primary process thinking. He is like other right-brained individuals of his time, except that he does exhibit some evidence of emerging conscious activity originating in his left brain. In my interpretation of Exodus, he evidences more than a modicum of consciousness. Perhaps I am being too generous!

Tradition ascribes the Book of Exodus to Moses himself. However, modern scholars place the actual writing of Exodus in Babylon during the 6th century BCE, with a final editing job in the post-exilic period the following century, which is the version we have.

One other thought on Moses and those venomous snakes. In the Greek sense, Moses' pole with its bronze serpent would represent a soterial object. The noun for soterial is soteria, meaning "salvation," "deliverance," or "providing a state of safety." Actually, the concept of the soteria is a staple of Greek philosophy. The very name of Socrates is said to be derived from *soter*, which means "savior."

Philo of Alexandria (20 BCE-50 CE), whose preoccupation was the blending of Greek philosophy with Judaism, found much to write about when it came to the soteria. For him, opposing soteria was a destructive force he called phthora, which would be equivalent to Freud's Thanatos or death wish and Pope John Paul ll's "culture of death."

To ward off phthora, we still find people resorting to an array of protective objects, such as potions and amulets, including the familiar rabbit's foot. Not any old rabbit's foot will do. It has to be the left hind foot, and the lagomorph has to be "prepared" during a full moon on a Friday the 13th by a cross-eyed man (eye color not specified).

The ancient Greeks would have accepted Moses' ophidian pole as a soteria. Another soteria, and perhaps the most popular soterial object in the world, is the Christian Cross. Soteriology, a Christian term, is the study of the doctrine of salvation, and for Christians, Jesus is the ultimate *soter*, as summarized in Titus 3:5–8.

CHAPTER 21

Moses' descent from the Mountain of God with the Ten Commandments marks the beginning of a long journey that will culminate centuries later in the birth of the world's first religion, Judaism. Here are just a couple of highlights of what transpired along the way, beginning with the story of Jonah.

The Book of Jonah could be entitled "Jonah and the Whale," for it is one whale of a story. Then again, "Jonah: What a Fish Story!" would do as well. Jonah's tale, one might say, is just about the biggest fish yarn ever. Well, maybe not. Carlo Collodi outdid the author of Jonah with *The Adventures of Pinocchio* (1883). During his various adventures and misadventures, Pinocchio is swallowed by the Terrible Dogfish, a dogfish-like sea monster (in

Hebrew, *tannin*, "sea monster") more than half a mile in length, not including its tail.

The largest fish in the Mediterranean is the giant white shark, made famous, or infamous, by Peter Benchley in his novel *Jaws* and Steven Spielberg's subsequent movie adaptation. Male great whites average 12 feet in length (females 15.5 feet) and are the largest predatory fish known, but not large enough to accommodate an average-size human comfortably or uncomfortably for a three-day sojourn, provided, of course, its guest survives its carnivorous jaws in the first place.

Perhaps a more hospitable host would be a blue whale, the leviathan of the deep. These sea creatures, the largest animals ever to have inhabited the earth, can grow to 90–100 feet in length, weigh as much as 100 tons, and digest 40 million (8,000 pounds) krill (small shrimplike crustaceans) a day, their dietary mainstay. Members of our species are not known to be even an occasional treat for these sea giants.

The blue whale, with a tongue the size of an elephant, has baleen (whalebone) bristles instead of teeth in its upper jaw that act like a comb. When the whale expels a mouthful of water it has ingested, the krell are retained on the bristles, which it then licks off with its tongue and swallows. (Baleen whales are thus "filter feeders.") However, as huge as the whale is, its esophageal opening is too narrow to admit anything as large as a grown human.

Those who read the Jonah text as word-for-word gospel will say that chapter 1 specifically mentions a large fish, not a whale. Of course, we know that the whale is a cetacean, that is, a marine mammal, not a fish, but the ancients didn't know that. They would have viewed a whale simply as a large fish (*dag gadol* in Hebrew), which is how the text reads. There was no word for "whale" in biblical times.

But is there any chance whatsoever that Jonah could have survived three days and three nights somewhere in the body of a whale? Memory of the first patient I saw as a medical student in 1961 at the Dundee Royal Infirmary in Scotland provided me with a possible answer.

He was a retired judge in his 70s, hale and hearty, but he lived with an inconvenient congenital defect: he had a pharyngeal pouch, an abnormal sac formed in the wall of his pharynx at the junction of the lower part of the throat and the esophagus. The elderly gentleman cheerfully demonstrated to the students gathered around him how he manipulated a specially designed silver spoon to scoop out food trapped in the pouch.

In baleen whales, such as the blue whale, but not in toothed whales, the pharynx resembles that of other mammals, and it is conceivable that Jonah could have been swallowed by a blue whale with a pharyngeal pouch. But it should be emphasized, a pharyngeal pouch is an anatomical anomaly rarely encountered in humans and probably never seen in a cetacean.

If events did happen as Jonah 1:17 states, and we are dealing with a blue whale, such a pouch, theoretically at least, could have been large enough to house Jonah for several days. He would have had to steel himself every time the whale opened its mouth to take in water and then expel it when (filter) feeding. Sleeping under such circumstances would be extremely difficult. Whether he would have enough oxygen when the leviathan was submerged is a key question. At least he would have been far enough removed from the sea-going beast's stomach with its gastric juice containing hydrochloric acid (pH 2–3, which is very strong) and the protein digesting enzyme pepsin so as not to wind up as so much chyme (digestive mush).

It should be noted that most species of whales can remain under water for 20 minutes before surfacing for air. The longest a human has held his breath under water is 19 minutes. Peter Colat, a Swiss free-diver, performed the feat in 2010, but he was allowed to breathe pure oxygen 10 minutes before his attempt. The biblical account does not mention if Jonah was a world-class free-diver.

Whatever his aquatic housing arrangement, Jonah was Mediterranean sea-going because he defied God. However, his defiance made obvious sense to him. Why would he want to preach a message of repentance to the Ninevites – that's what he was charged by God to do – when the might of Assyria would soon enough destroy his beloved Israel?

A prophet hears the word of God and transmits His message to the people. He also has the gift of prophecy – the ability to catch a glimpse of the future. Jonah knew what would befall Israel in the second half of the 8th century BCE: the Assyrian horde would descend upon the Northern Kingdom (in 722 BCE), and its 10 tribes would vanish into oblivion.

He was between the devil and the deep blue sea – or as they say nowadays, between a rock and a hard place[86] – forced to bring spiritual aid and comfort to the detestable inhabitants of Nineveh, or defy heaven and suffer God's displeasure. Emotionally distraught as he was, he nevertheless managed to board a cargo ship at Joppa on the Mediterranean headed west – Nineveh was in the opposite direction – to Tarshish beyond the Pillars of Hercules (Strait of Gibraltar), symbolically, the ends of the earth.

Jonah's ministry is dated to the first half of the 8th century BCE, and his visit to Nineveh – he eventually gets there – can be narrowed down to about 757 or 756. Jeroboam ll was on the throne of Israel from 786–746, and Assur-pan lll ruled over Assyria

---

86 When I was in high school during the first lustrum (one of John Wayne's favorite words) of the 1940s, the expression was the more literary "between Scylla and Charybdis."

(772–755) from his throne in Assur (or Ashur), the Neo-Assyrian capital, located about fifty or so miles downstream from Nineveh on the west bank of the Tigris.

How Jonah got to Nineveh from way out in the Mediterranean heading west is an intriguing tale. Three days out of port a storm came up the likes of which the ship's crew of old salts had never experienced. Jonah, trying to hide from God's wrath, as represented by the storm, took refuge in the belly of the ship curled up in the fetal position – back to the safety of mother's womb – but even there God found him. "And he [Jonah] said unto them [the crew], I am an Hebrew, and I fear the LORD, the God of heaven, which hath made the sea and the dry land" (Jonah 1:9). He has himself thrown overboard to save the ship and its crew, and the storm ceases. And now, between the sea and dry land, is the nuts and bolts of the Jonah story.

CHAPTER 22

As a note of explanation, I do not disguise the fact that my approach to the Book of Jonah is eisegetical. Eisegesis refers to reading one's own ideas into a biblical text. The opposite would be exegetical, where exegesis designates limiting oneself to traditional Bible commentary.

Actually, the Jonah story can be seen from several perspectives. For instance, the book is full of paronomasia, that is, word play. Oscar Wilde, the undisputed lord of the pun, dripped bon mots: "Immanuel doesn't pun, he Kant." In *The Importance of Being*

Earnest, Wilde uses the name Ernest as the pun in a comedic farce of double identity and dualistic themes to mock the hypocrisy of Late Victorian Society. Other examples of paronomasia: there's a beauty salon in London called "Curl Up and Dye," and the city also sports a barber shop named "Al's Clip Joint."

For Baruch Halpern (*The First Historians: The Hebrew Bible and History*) and Richard Elliott Friedman (*Who Wrote the Bible?*), the Book of Jonah "is a rich, almost baroque sampler of paronomastic techniques…From the instances of word-repetition and word-play…it should be clear that the art of sound and language characterizes the book of Jonah." (Quoted from their article, "Composition and Paronomasia in the Book of Jonah," *Hebrew Annual Review*, vol. 4, 1980.) My focus regarding the Book of Jonah lies elsewhere.

Two points to bear in mind in thinking about life in the 8th century BCE are: people didn't distinguish between the natural and supernatural realms and gods dominated their lives. These two issues were noted for life in Moses' time, the 13th century BCE. The one significant change: man had long ceased to be bicameral. Nevertheless, a few individuals still heard the voices of their ancient gods. In Israel, they were called prophets, and Jonah was one of them.

To resume where I left off at the end of the previous chapter, after three days and three nights of incommodious and distressing life within his sea-going host, Jonah found himself spewed out upon dry land somewhere along the Phoenician coast near one of the city-states – Tyre, Sidon, Byblos – north of Joppa, his starting point. Those who observed him as he emerged from the sea were spellbound. To them, he was none other than the fish-god Dagon, half man, half fish, but now morphed into full human form.

Jonah was quick to disavow such an explanation for his dramatic appearance, repeating again and again that he was, like them, just an ordinary mortal and that it was his god, the LORD God of Israel, that is, YHVH, who had delivered him from a sea monster that had swallowed him. His listeners would smile benignly, afraid to get too close to the human-appearing form they saw as Dagon.

He now began the journey by camel caravan to Nineveh, some 500 miles to the east, which would take about three weeks. Just as the fish in a good fish story grows bigger and bigger with each retelling, so did the aura of the fish-man Jonah expand with each passing day. By the time he arrived, the Ninevites, fully informed by fleet-footed messengers days in advance of his coming, were already in a mind-set to do anything their fish-god would demand of them.

He was in what we would call a win-win situation. He kept telling his listeners that it was his god, the LORD God, who had commissioned him to preach a message of redemption to the Ninevites, but it seemed as though every last denizen of the city had heard how he, Dagon, their fish-god, had emerged from the waters of the sea and was coming to Nineveh.

"God knows what He is doing," he murmured. "He guided me through this alien and hostile country to my destination. I serve the God of Hosts, not some water deity. But if I must breach the walls of Nineveh as Dagon in order to deliver His message, so be it."

His euphoria would be short-lived because, as we know, his heart and mind were never in the mission. Jonah, although a prophet of Israel, is not considered a monotheist at the time of his arrival in Nineveh; instead, he is to be seen as a henotheist, since he acknowledges the existence of the Ninevites' fish-god Dagon (and most likely other gods). But Dagon isn't mentioned in the biblical account of Jonah, you argue. Well, he should have been included, but the writer of the Book of Jonah condensed his story into a few pages and failed to mention anything about Dagon.

Then again, he may have been included in earlier versions but was subsequently edited out.

Jonah didn't have to do much. He stood in the city's central square and bellowed: "Forty more days and Nineveh will be destroyed." His voice carried deep into the city, and his words were relayed still farther by others. Everyone comprehended his message (delivered in Aramaic, the lingua franca of the Fertile Crescent).

They understood and, in biblical speak, harkened unto his voice, including the king (not King Assur-pan lll in Assur, the capital, but a vassal king), who covered himself with sackcloth and ashes (a sign of submission).[87]

Their contriteness was genuine, but it didn't impress the impassive Jonah. His duty was to deliver God's message – as His prophet (or in the guise of Dagon) – which he had now done. Nothing more was required of him, he reasoned.

In Jonah 1:9, the prophet says: "I will pay that that I have vowed." We do not know what he had vowed when he was in distress in the interior of the great fish. It is not uncommon to call upon God in time of trouble but to forget Him when deliverance comes. But as already noted in the previous chapter, there is another explanation for Jonah's reluctance to do more: he didn't want to participate in Assyria's restoration to power.

The Hebrew for contrite is *dakka*, which also connotes "crushed, crippled, or broken." The connotation of *dakka* adequately summarizes the mental state in Assyria during the 760s and 750s. While Israel enjoyed unprecedented prosperity under Jeroboam ll (reigned 786–746), Assyria was stagnating, especially during the reign of Assur-dan lll (772–755). A plague in 765 devastated the country, which was followed by a second widespread plague in 759. In between, on June 15, 763, there was a solar eclipse. This

---

87   Also as a token of mourning.

natural event, in the 8th century BCE, was considered an unfavorable omen, presaging disaster and destruction. In fact, during the eclipse there was a revolt in the capital, Assur. Jonah's arrival in Nineveh occurred toward the end of Assur-dan lll's kingship, perhaps 757 or 756.

Jonah, against his better judgment, had saved the Ninevites, a nasty, cruel people, at least for the moment. He built a ramshackle shack and waited to see how long their reformation would last, while cursing them repeatedly under his breath. God took pity on his grumbling servant in his wretched shack beneath a broiling sun and caused a castor-bean plant to grow overnight whose broad leaves would at least afford him shading from the torrid sun. However, seeing that His prophet just sat on his hands and did nothing, that is, did not follow up on his initial success, He destroyed the castor-oil plant and left the disgruntled, sulking Jonah to squirm in the noon-day sun.

With four words in Aramaic (eight in English: "Forty more days and Nineveh will be destroyed"), he had electrified the Ninevites, who had never seen their god, Dagon, in the flesh and now were awed and befuddled to encounter him as a syncretic Dagon/Yahweh. Their bewilderment, however, would be short-lived. First, they rejected the idea of Jonah's foreign Hebrew god as having anything to do with their lives, and then they realized that this faint-hearted, contemptible individual had nothing to do with their all-powerful god Dagon.

Jonah, not surprisingly, was relieved that things were coming apart. The Ninevites' rehabilitation lasted only forty days (according to the Talmud), and then they were back to what they had been. A new king, Tiglath-Pileser lll (ruled 745–727) would rise up and reestablish Assyrian hegemony in the Mideast. His sons, Shalmaneser V and Sargon ll, would conquer the Northern

Kingdom in 722–721 and carry off its 10 tribes, the Ten Lost Tribes, proving Jonah's vision of the future had been accurate.

So, how much of the Book of Jonah is historical and how much is fiction? The big fish sequence at the beginning of the tale has to be considered a fish story, ranking near the top of the list of craniate sea animal whoppers. Some of the material in the book is historical. For instance, the solar eclipse of 763 BCE is well documented. Even the prophet Amos, a contemporary of Jonah, makes mention of it (Amos 8:9).

Jonah is listed among the minor prophets, and that by itself lends credence to his historicity. Curiously, however, the only proof of his actual existence is to be found in 2 Kings 14:25: "[Jeroboam ll] restored the coast of Israel from the entering of Hamath unto the sea of the plain, according to the word of the LORD God of Israel, which he spake by the hand of his servant Jonah, the son of Amittai, the prophet, which was of Gathhepher." Clarifying the verse, Jeroboam regained territory east of the Jordan lost to the Syrians, from Hamath in the Orontes valley southward to the Dead Sea.

In a previous passage, 2 Kings 9:1–6, the prophet Elisha dispatched one of his young disciples to Ramoth- Gilead to anoint an army officer, Jehu son of Jehoshaphat, king of Israel. The year was 842 BCE, and the young disciple was Jonah, not actually named in the text, but tradition has him acting as the anointer of Jehu.[88] The young prophet was probably in his early 20s at the time.[89]

---

88   In 1 Kings 19:16, it is Elijah who anoints Jehu king of Israel and then Elisha as his successor.

89   Elisha was too old for the task and chose a young, nimble acolyte to go in his place, adding that when he had anointed Jehu: "Then open the door, and flee, and tarry not" (2 Kings 9:3). He, of course, knew the coup d'etat would be followed by a bloodbath.

Jonah, as already noted, arrived in Ninevah around 756, which means he was past 120 when he had his encounter with Mocha Dick[90] and subsequently bobbed up and down on the waters of the Mediterranean for three days and three nights before reaching dry land. All I can say about that remarkable centenarian is: "Stout fellow!"

The Book of Jonah contains only four short chapters covering a little more than three pages. Chapter 4, somewhat incomplete and hazy in construction – reflecting, I would venture to say, poor editing by the scribes – ends with God explaining to Jonah why He spared Nineveh with its 120,000 persons "that cannot discern between their right hand and their left hand." By that, God was saying that they couldn't distinguish between right and wrong. (Shades of Sodom and Gomorrah – and of half of postmodern America!)

God Himself is unchanging, and this bit of the Jonah story illustrates an important change, or advance, in the development of Jewish consciousness and the Jewish conceptualization of God from the time of Abraham, circa 2000 BCE, when the biblical patriarch couldn't persuade El Shaddai not to destroy Sodom and Gomorrah.

Despite their human shortcomings, the Ninevites were part of God's creation. The author of the Book of Jonah had made his point: God's love was not restricted to His Chosen People but was universal (one step short of seeing God Himself as being universal). But that's not the only point of the book.

---

90   The 70-foot-long male sperm whale that served as the inspiration for Herman Melville's *Moby Dick*. First spotted near Mocha Island off the coast of Chile, Mocha Dick destroyed at least 20 ships and had 20 harpoons in his carcass when finally killed.

There is no doubt that the Lord God of Israel scored a triumph at Nineveh, even though some deception was needed to get His prophet into the city. Having Jonah pass as the fish-god Dagon does seem...well, unkosher, but God does have a sense of humor.

It was a bold move on the part of Yahweh to send His prophet deep into such an alien lair as Assyria, whose inhabitants had a reputation for barbarism and xenophobia. To make things even more difficult, the country at the time was enduring natural disasters and economic depression, and life for foreigners was unsettling and even precarious.

And He had succeeded with a wizened neurotic, proving what Paul centuries later would summarize with these words he wrote to his church in Corinth: "God hath chosen the weak things of the world to confound the things which are mighty" (1 Corinthians 1:27).

Jeroboam ll (ruled 786–746 BCE) had none of Ashur-dan lll's problems. Sometimes referred to as "the last of the great kings of Israel," he was a talented organizer and capable field commander. During his reign, Israel reached the height of economic prosperity, built on trade in olive oil, wine, and horses with Assyria and Egypt; and he extended Israel's borders to their former boundaries under Solomon, as already noted.

Assyrian aggression toward Israel began around 740. In 722, Samaria, the nation's capital, fell to Sargon ll after a 3-year siege begun by Shalmaneser V. The peace with Assyria Jeroboam had hoped for when Jonah traveled to Nineveh in 757 (or 756), although off to a good start, quickly fizzled out. Israel would now cease to exist as a nation.

There is still a loose end to the story of Jonah: Dagon. The fish-god figures in Jewish history even before the time of the kings. In the 11th century BCE, the strongman Samson, blinded and reduced to grinding grain for his Philistine captors, brought down their filled-to-the-rafters temple to Dagon in Gaza, perishing as well in a final act of atonement.[91]

In the 11th century BCE, Dagon was a god of grain and considered a symbol of fertility. In Hebrew, *dag* means "fish" and *dagan*, "grain." Furthermore, archeologists have found sculptures of the fish-god in Nineveh; so Dagon worship was not limited to the Mediterranean coast, as had been thought for so long.

Dagon was only one of many deities in an elaborate pantheon Ninevites worshipped. The goddess Nina was in charge of fish and fishing and was also the mother of the mermaids. (Dagon was often depicted as a merman.) Nina was also a variant spelling of Ninua, Akkadian for the place name Nineveh. In cuneiform, Nina (Aramaic , *nuna*, meaning "fish") is represented as a fish within a house. In Akkadian, *nunu* is the word for "fish." Related to it is *ninus*,[92] which means "the residence of Nimrod," the legendary founder of Nineveh, and Assyria is "the land of Nimrod."

All in all, there is something fishy about the name "Nineveh." Nineveh, one may say, is Fishtown, Fishville, Fishburg, even Fish City. From its beginning to its end, from the fish that swallowed Jonah to Nineveh/Fishtown, the Book of Jonah is a fish tale. (And from a purely literary perspective, it's loaded with paronomasia).

There is a takeaway: Jonah could have been a big fish in a big pond, but because of personal shortcomings, he ended up being remembered as a minnow in a fish bowl.

---

91 Samson died c.1078 BCE. Saul's years are given as c.1080 – c.1012. He may have reigned as king for 20 or perhaps 22 years, but as Israeli archeologist Israel Finkelstein has pointed out, there is no reliable evidence to support these numbers. His reign marked the end of Israelite tribal life and the beginning of nationhood.

92 The historian Strabo refers to Nineveh as Ninus in his *Geography*.

CHAPTER 23

Before there was a Babylonian captivity (or Babylonian exile), there was an Asssyrian captivity (Assyrian exile) during which thousands of Israelites were resettled in Assyria as captives. History remembers them as the Ten Lost Tribes. Forced deportation was a strategy developed by Tiglath-Pileser lll, king of the Neo-Assyrian Empire (745–727 BCE), to discourage uprisings against Assyrian rule. His name may not be familiar to many readers, but during his lifetime he conquered most of the known world, at least to the Assyrians. When he died, he was succeeded by his son Shalmaneser V (ruled 727–722 BCE), who expanded the Assyrian captivity. With his death, his brother, Sargon ll, finished the "resettlement" of the Israelites.

Sargon was succeeded by his son, Sennacherib, who ruled Assyria from 705 to 681 BCE. In Akkadian, his name is spelled *Sin-ahhi-eriba*, meaning "Sin has replaced his brothers," where Sin is the same Moon-god who figured so prominently in the Exodus saga.

As Egypt had to contend with the Hittites during the time of Moses, so did Sennacherib have his own nemesis in Babylon. For much of his time on the throne, he was engrossed in the so-called "Babylonian problem," Babylon's refusal to accept Assyrian dominance, which he finally solved by destroying the city in 689 BCE. He is also remembered for having invaded Judah and having rebuilt Nineveh. His "Palace without Rival" would rival Windsor Castle, built by William the Conqueror in the late 11th century CE. Sennacherib's palace included the actual Hanging Gardens of

135

Babylon,[93] one of the Seven Wonders of the Ancient World, for a long time thought to have been built by Nebuchadnezzar ll for his homesick wife, Amytis of Media.[94]

Before proceeding to the centerpiece of this chapter, which is Sennacherib's invasion of Judah and Lord Byron's narrative poem, "The Destruction of Sennacherib," based on the biblical account found in 2 Kings 18–19, I would like to say a few words about Byron.

A number of years ago I gave a talk on George Gordon Byron (1788–1824) entitled "Lord Byron and History." I spent some time describing his involvement in the Greek struggle for independence against the Ottoman Turks, culminating in his death from a fever in April 1824 just as his Byron Brigade was about to launch an attack on the strategic fortress of Lepanto at the mouth of the Gulf of Corinth. To this day, Lord Byron is revered as a national hero in Greece.

Most of my talk dealt with his poem "The Destruction of Sennacherib," one of a number of Byronic poems set to music by Isaac Nathan[95] in his "Hebrew Melodies," a collaboration that turned out to be financially profitable for both of them. Some of Nathan's melodies were incorporated into the liturgy used in London's Sephardic synagogues. Byron's "She Walks in Beauty," for example, was written to be sung to the mystical hymn *Lecha Dodi* ("Come My Beloved"), written by the 16th century kabbalist Rabbi Shlomo Halevy Alkabetz and considered one of the

---

93   The Hanging Gardens of Babylon were really the Hanging Gardens of Nineveh.

94   Today's Azerbaijan, Kurdistan, and parts of Kermanshah in Iran (considered one of the cradles of prehistoric culture).

95   The English-born son of a Polish synagogue cantor, he referred to the LORD God of Israel as "the most High and Wonderful Geometrician of the Universe."

finest illustrations of religious poetry. Isaac Nathan subsequently emigrated to Australia, where he earned the title of "Australia's first composer."

Sennacherib's reign as king of Assyria (705–681) was sandwiched between two monumental historic events: the Assyrian annihilation of Israel in 721 BCE and the Babylonian conquest of Judah in 586 BCE. "The Destruction of Sennacherib," composed in anapestic tetrameter (q.v.), is Byron's poetic version of 2 Kings 18–19.

King Hezekiah had allied himself with Egypt against Assyria, and in 701 BCE Sennacherib, with an army of over 200,000 men, invaded Judah: "The Assyrian came down like the wolf on the fold," is Byron's opening line in "The Destruction of Sennacherib." The Assyrian king devastated the countryside on his march to Jerusalem, including the capture and plunder of Lachish, Judah's second largest city, carrying off thousands of Judahites (Jews) for "resettlement."

There are two versions of what happened next: the biblical, which is the version Lord Byron follows, and the Assyrian. Sennacherib's army surrounded Jerusalem and was ready to begin the assault on the city, waiting only for daybreak (according to the poem). But when the sun came up, the terrain lay strewn with Assyrian dead, 185,000 in all, the Bible states, without an arrow being shot or a spear thrown from within Jerusalem's walls. The biblical account says Sennacherib was defeated "by the angel of the Lord." We would say a pestilence, perhaps cholera or typhus, decimated the Assyrian force, but certainly not in one night as the poetic version has it: "Like the leaves of the forest when autumn hath blown/That host on the morrow lay withered and strown."

The Assyrian version was quite different. Sennacherib's Prism, a six-sided prism standing 38 centimeters high and 14 centimeters wide dated to 689 BCE, included the statement: "Hezekiah himself I shut up in Jerusalem, his capital city, like a bird in a cage." Sennacherib exacted heavy tribute from an apologetic and contrite Hezekiah and returned victorious to Nineveh.

For Hezekiah, whose name in Hebrew means "God is my strength," and the Judahites, it was a great victory for their god, Yahweh, over the Assyrian gods, expressed in the poem's final two lines: "And the might of the Gentile, unsmote by the sword/Hath melted like wax in the glance of the Lord." This is the way people of that time continued to view reality: gods were still involved in the outcome of human events.

The prophet Isaiah had encouraged Hezekiah to remain strong in the face of Sennacherib's threats to destroy Jerusalem and carry off its inhabitants, as his grandfather, Tiglath-Pileser, uncle, Shalmaneser, and father, Sargon ll, had done with Samaria[96] and the Israelites. "And he prayed before the LORD, and said, O LORD God of Israel...thou art the God, even thou alone, of all the kingdoms of the earth; thou hast made heaven and earth" (2 Kings 19:15).

And the LORD God of Israel did deliver the Jews out of the hands of Sennacherib, who retreated back to Nineveh with the remnant of his army, reminiscent of Napoleon and what was left of his *Grande Armee* retreating from Moscow in the Russian winter of 1812.

But 2 Kings 19:15 is itself a redaction, a bit of historical reorganization. Some later editor put those monotheistic words in the mouth of Hezekiah. The time is the tail end of the 8th century BCE, and at that stage of their religious development the Jews were at best henotheistic. The "monotheistic movement" that would

---

96   The city of Samaria was the capital of the Northern Kingdom (also known as the Kingdom of Israel and the Kingdom of Samaria) in the 9th and 8th centuries BCE.

culminate in the crystallization of Judaism would have to wait until the time of Deutero-Isaiah in the 6th century BCE.

CHAPTER 24

It just so happens the Bible furnishes a third version of the siege of Jerusalem. "Now Sennacherib received a report that Tirhakah, the king of Cush, was marching out to fight against him..." (2 Kings 19:9, NIV). The New Living Translation identifies Tirhakah as the king of Ethiopia, as do the KJV and several other translations. The Good News Translation blends – or blurs – identities with: "the Egyptian army, led by King Tirhakah of Ethiopia, was coming to attack" the Assyrians. That was enough to encourage "the wolf on the fold" to withdraw to his lair in Nineveh.

The Hebrew word *kush*, spelled Cush in English, doesn't translate readily for modern readers. It used to indicate Ethiopia, but over the past half century "Nubia" and "Sudan," or "northern Sudan," appear more frequently in the literature. Linguistics is not my area of expertise, far from it, and I had better let this issue go.

There is a problem with chronology. Taharkah, also written as Taharka and Taharqa, reigned as pharaoh from 690 to 664 BCE. Sennacherib moved on Judah in 701 BCE when Neferkare Shabaka, the third Kushite pharaoh of the 25th dynasty of Egypt, was on the throne (705–690 BCE). It seems we should be talking about Shabaka, not Taharkah, coming to Hezekiah's aid.

Much to my surprise, Byron's poem has touched more people than I ever realized. Mark Twain refers to "The Destruction of

Sennacherib" in *The Adventures of Tom Sawyer* and elsewhere in his writings. Ogden Nash, poet of yesteryear known for his humorous rhymes, parodied Byron with: "Now then, this particular Assyrian, the one whose cohorts were gleaming in purple and gold,/Just what does the poet mean when he says he came down like a wolf on the fold?" Techno-thriller novelist Tom Clancy begins his *The Sum of All Fears* with: "Like a wolf on the fold."

I first read "The Destruction of Sennacherib" about seventy years ago in an English literature course at college. The poem was included in the textbook we used primarily to illustrate anapestic tetrameter: two unstressed syllables followed by a third stressed syllable, with four anapests to a line. "And the widows of Ashur are loud in their wail,/And the idols are broke in the temple of Baal..." The words literally sing. As noted above, the poem, along with a number of others by Lord Byron, was written as lyrics to go with synagogal music composed by Isaac Nathan.

From the point of view of those Jews who lived through the siege of Jerusalem in 701 BCE, the story boils down to Yahweh and how one of His angels saved Jerusalem. The poet's wording: "For the Angel of Death spread his wings on the blast,/And breathed in the face of the foe as he passed." According to the biblical text (2 Kings 19:35), the Angel of Death breathed in the face of 185,000 Assyrian soldiers. In Jewish lore, the Angel of Death is also referred to as Abaddon (The Destroyer) and Azrael. And then there is Michael, one of the seven archangels, who, according to the Talmud (Midrash Rabah 18:5), destroyed Sennacherib's army.

Now and again we find fixed dates in history, that is, dates we can rely on as being accurate, such as the June 15, 763 BCE eclipse of the sun, which astronomers can verify with precision. When it comes to Sennacherib's invasion of Judah, well, it occurred in *approximately* 701 BCE, which is about as close as historians can come to figuring the time of this particular event. But how accurate is the biblical count of 185,000 dead Assyrians? Even as an estimate it seems exaggeratedly high. This is not at all out of place for the time and place. Writers in the ancient Middle East had a tendency to inflate numbers and hyperbolize facts. In 2 Samuel 24:9, Joab reported to King David that in Israel there were 800,000 "valiant men that drew the sword" and 500,000 in Judah, well over a million fighting men, at a time when the world's population was about 50 million.

"And Saul [born c. 1080 BCE, died c. 1012 BCE] gathered the people together, and numbered them in Telaim, two hundred thousand footmen, and ten thousand men in Judah" (1 Samuel 15:4). His army of 210,000 would have been the largest in the world! Telaim was Saul's base in Judah, from where he would launch a counter-attack on the Amalekites under King Agag, who were raiding Judah.

"And Saul smote the Amalekites from Havilah until thou comest to Shur, that is over against Egypt," which is like saying figuratively: "from here to the moon" (1 Samuel 15:7).

"And he took Agag the king of the Amalekites alive, and *utterly* [my italics] destroyed all the people with the edge of the sword" (1 Sam. 15:8).

The literature of the Near East, not just the Bible, is replete with accounts that include "utterly or completely destroy" and related obliteration wording. In an earlier passage, 1 Samuel 15:3, Samuel says to Saul: "Now go and smote Amalek, and utterly destroy all that they have, and spare them not; but slay both men and women, infant and suckling, ox and sheep, camel and ass."

By the time we get to Esther, the Jewish queen of the Persian king Ahasuerus/Xerxes, there shouldn't be a single Amalekite or Amalekite ass still alive, but that's not apparently the case. Here we encounter Haman "the Agagite" (Esther 3:1) continuing the ancestral conflict in the form of a vendetta against the Jews.

In Jeremiah 25:9, God says Nebuchadressar will conquer "all those nations round about, and will utterly destroy them, and make them…an everlasting desolation," because, in the case of the Judahites, they had forsaken their God and had fallen into idolatry, immolating their children as offerings to Baal. Interestingly, the Babylonian king is presented to us as God's servant, or we might say, His avenging angel.

Nineveh is described in Jonah 3:3 as a very large city "of three days journey." Someone walking at a leisurely pace of 2–3 miles an hour for 8 hours, the camel caravan pace, would cover 48–72 miles (let's say 60 miles, averaging the two) in 3 days. A city of such size would be a megalopolis. The author exaggerates, to say the least. Depicting Nineveh as 60 miles in breadth is an example of what is referred to as Semitic hyperbole, an oft-used device of biblical writers and editors.

Although not the megalopolis the author would have us believe Nineveh actually was, it nevertheless was large, covering 1850 acres, second in size in the ancient Near East to Babylon with 2500 acres.

Hyperbolic language is especially evident in Joshua and Deuteronomy, where you encounter such phases as: "leave alive none that breathes" (Deut. 20:16) and "put all inhabitants to the sword" (Deut. 13:15, Joshua 8:24, 6:21). Yet survivors pop up later in Judges and Deuteronomy. Such hyperbolized expressions are found throughout the Hebrew Bible and New Testament and are to be considered SOP, or more to the point, SLOP, standard literary operating procedure.

The use of hyperbole, furthermore, is characteristic of the writing style everywhere in the Near East at the time. Sennacherib writes about a successful campaign: "The soldiers of [the Babylonian city of] Hirimme, dangerous enemies, I cut down with the sword; and not one escaped" (quoted from Sennacherib's

Prism). In *The 10 Year Annals of Mursilli*, Muwatalli's father, King Mursilli ll (ruled the Hittite Empire from 1322 to 1295 BCE), recorded that he made "Mt. Asharpaya empty [of Kaskaeans]" and the "mountains of Tarikarimu empty [of Kaskaeans]...And I came back to Hattusa." Ramesses ll's son, Merneptah, in the Merneptah Stele (c. 1230 BCE), proclaimed: "Israel is wasted, his seed is not." After his successful revolt against Israel (c. 850 BCE), King Mesha of Moab, as recorded in the Moabite Stone, proclaims: "Israel has utterly perished for always." Not so again! The Northern Kingdom would fall to the Assyrians in 721 BCE, which was about 130 years after Mesha's boast, but would rise again as the modern state of Israel 2669 years later.

Jesus of Nazareth furnishes us an example of 1st-century CE Semitic hyperbole with his "judge not, that ye be not judged" metaphor in Matthew 7:3: "And why beholdest thou the mote that is in thy brother's eye, but considerest not the beam that is in thine own eye?" Here Jesus attacks the hypocrites who attack others for slight flaws while overlooking their own larger short-comings. Or as we are wont to say today: "People in glass houses shouldn't throw stones."

CHAPTER 25

My neighbor and her 5-year-old granddaughter were getting ready to go to church, and I greeted them, as I did many a Sunday morning, with the words: "Give my regards to my good friend, Rabbi Jesus.

What my fellow Jews know and understand about Rabbi Jesus is meager at best. Likewise, Christians, who know a good deal about the divine Jesus, have a limited familiarity about him as a Jew.

Jesus was a key figure in the rabbinical world of early 1st-century Jewry. But when it came to writing the Jewish history of that period, his name was stricken from the scrolls, much in the manner that Ramesses ll had Moses' name removed from all monuments and inscriptions associated with his early life and career as an Egyptian general.

Jesus has been a major focus throughout my long life, which, since I am Jewish to the core, may seem paradoxical. In my spiritual quest, I draw upon resources from both Judaism and Christianity without compromising my Jewish identity. For Jews, the dividing line is stated clearly in Isaiah 43:11: "I, even I, am the LORD; *and beside me there is no savior.*" Yahweh is the only God Jews acknowledge.

Still, I can read from Isaiah and the same day, perhaps at the same sitting, I might read about St. Josemaría Escrivá (1902–1975), founder of Opus Dei. Escrivá, by the way, believed there should be a Jewish-Christian dialogue. Rabbi Angel Kreiman, former chief rabbi of Chile, said of him: "He calls to mind the Talmudic tradition...That which most likens his teaching to Judaism is the vocation of man to serve God through creative work, perfecting creation every day...."In Hebrew, this is referred to as *tikkun olam.*

I can appreciate St. Ignatius of Antioch's statement: "It is a beautiful thing to die to the world for the Lord, so as to rise in him." Whether spelled as Lord, as in this case, or LORD, the Jewish rendition in English, for Jews, the name is Yahweh, and He is the only savior.

The basic outline of the life of Jesus is clear-cut enough. Jesus was born into a first-century Jewish household, lived the life of a dedicated rabbi, and died a Jew, accused of sedition by Judea's Roman occupiers.

But already we are into disputed waters. Jewish and Christian traditions view the events leading up to Jesus' crucifixion differently. The Christian position, as recorded in the Gospels, is that "the Jews" – actually, it was the High Priest and his minions, not the populace – instigated his death with their charge of blasphemy. However, the point is moot, because in these pages I deal only with the life of Jesus, not his death.

Looking at Jesus through Jewish eyes can also furnish us a new way of thinking about James, the brother of Jesus. Jesus had three other brothers – Joseph, Simeon and Judas, as well as two unnamed sisters. Simon Peter, not a blood relation, may have been given "the keys of the kingdom of heaven by Jesus" (Matthew 16:19), but his actual role was as chief minister of the early Jerusalem Church.

Jesus' resurrection solidified his identity as Messiah ("the anointed one," that is, the king of Israel) in the minds of his followers. While waiting for the Parousia, the return, or second coming, of Jesus,[97] his nearest blood relation, James, served as his earthly stand-in. The Parousia was expected at any moment, as we find in the epistle of James 5:7–8: "Be patient, brothers, until the Lord's coming…the Lord's coming is near."

A key point: there is nothing in the epistle of James (dated to sometime before 62 CE), nor in the historical record to indicate that during those early years the members of the "Jesus movement," as the early Nazarene community was called, ever thought of Jesus as divine. James never considered his brother to be God, but did, conceivably, see him as the Messiah.

The New Testament downplays the role of Jesus' family in the development of the early Jewish-Christian community and

---

97   The wording in Christianity is the Second Coming of Christ.

ignores the fact that the movement[98] was monarchical. James ran things in Jerusalem, its center. Simon Peter took Jesus' message to Rome, which would become the hub of a new religion. Jesus himself played no direct role in the establishment of Christianity. Much would be said in his name, but in his lifetime, Jesus focused on his teaching, *Malchut Shamayim*, kingdom theology; secondarily, he was involved in a struggle against Rome, which he considered the devil's lair – the Evil Empire.

James was martyred in 62 CE. His brother Simeon then took over the leadership of the Jerusalem Church and for four decades was the most significant figure in the Jewish-Christian movement. He was followed after his death by Judas (Jude). Saint Hegesippus, a convert from Judaism, writing in the 2nd century, mentions that the emperor Domitian (81–96 CE) was alert to any possible new Jewish revolt. He had Judas' grandsons, Zoker (shortened form of Zechariah) and James, brought to Rome, where they convinced him they were simple, hard-working farmers with no kingly aspirations.

Judas, the youngest of Jesus' brothers (or half-brothers) would have been in his nineties when Simeon was crucified under Trajan[99] in 106 CE. With the death of Judas some years later, the "Jewish royal family" would fade from history.

---

98 During those early years, the "Jesus movement" was also called the Way.

99 Medieval Christian theologians judged Trajan (reigned 98–117 CE) to be a "virtuous pagan."

CHAPTER 26

No one in history has had more written about him than Jesus of Nazareth. Yet hardly anything is actually known about the man and his life. What is written about his divinity is a separate matter, a non-Jewish matter, which I do not address here; my focus in these pages is on the Jewish Jesus, not the Christianized Jesus.

Thus, Jews can approach the Christian scriptures from their own perspective. For instance, in Mark 13:1, Jesus and his disciples are in Jerusalem, and one of the disciples stands in awe of the Temple's massive stone structure.

Jesus says, "Not one stone here will be left on another, every one will be thrown down" (Mark 13:2).

Is this a prophecy of the destruction of the Temple, or did Mark, writing in the 70s, add this to his Gospel? If the Gospel were written before the bloody Jewish-Roman War, which started in 66, is this an interpolation, a later add-on to the pericope? (A pericope is an episode or story unit in the synoptic Gospels.)[100]

Consider Matthew 27:25, the scene where the Jerusalem mob is shouting for Barabbas' release and Jesus' condemnation: "Then answered all the people, and said, 'His blood be on us, and on our children.'"

Matthew, notwithstanding this statement, was the most Jewish of the three Jewish Gospel writers (Mark, Matthew, and John). Luke, the fourth, was a gentile.

The statement is most likely a later interpolation. Matthew's Gospel as we have it was written after the war (66–73 CE), probably in the 80s or 90s, when anti-Jewish sentiment among Roman

---

100 From Gk. *synoptikos*, "taking a general or comprehensive view," referring to the Gospels ascribed to Mark, Matthew, and Luke.

administrators and troops was still high. It would have been advisable for Jewish followers of Jesus and those already referred to as Christians – the distinction still not clear in the minds of the Romans – to placate these foreign occupiers of Judea. That particular shout from the mob – "His blood be on us, and on our children" --has resounded down through the centuries and has been interchangeable with "Christ killers!"

There is a certain irony in this because Matthew 20:18–19 relates that Jesus was going to Jerusalem to be mocked and *crucified* [my emphasis]: "Behold, we are going up to Jerusalem, and the Son of Man will be betrayed to the chief priests and to the scribes; and they will condemn Him to death, and deliver Him to the Gentiles to mock and to scourge and to crucify [Him]." Incidentally, this is the first time Jesus mentions the way he will die – by crucifixion.

Both the High Priest Caiaphas with his fellow quislings and the Roman power structure wanted his death, which Jesus himself saw as necessary, for it was his mission to suffer for the salvation of Jews and non-Jews alike, according to the Gospels. Therefore, both were to have a hand in his death, and in his death would be their redemption.

In recent years a number of Christian writers have attempted to search out the historical Jesus and make him sound more Jewish, or at least a little Jewish. Retired Episcopal Bishop of Newark, New Jersey, John Shelby Spong, author of *Liberating the Gospels*, subtitled his book *Reading the Bible with Jewish Eyes*. His visual acuity is not 20/20 Jewish and his depth perception does not penetrate very far into the Jewish Jesus. As Martin Buber once commented: "We Jews know Jesus in a way – in the impulses and emotions of his essential Jewishness – that remains inaccessible to the Gentile subject to him."

Philip Yancey (*The Jesus I Never Knew*) writes that as a boy growing up in Atlanta, he "knew that Jews had something to do with World War II, but I had heard little about the Holocaust. Certainly, these people had no relation to my Jesus."

Likewise, Bishop Spong writes that as a boy "not only did I not understand that Jesus was Jewish, but it never occurred to me to assume that his disciples were Jewish either." That is, except for Judas Iscariot, whom he pictured as dark, sinister, and evil, characteristics, he adds, "I had been taught were typical of the Jews."

To illustrate just how Jewish Jesus was, turn to Matthew 15:21–28. In this pericope, a Canaanite woman beseeches Jesus to free her daughter tormented by a demon. Jesus ignores her repeated pleas and finally says, "I was sent only to the lost sheep of the house of Israel."

She persists with her entreaties, and Jesus says, "It is not right to take the food of the children and throw it to the dogs." The poor alien woman has been humiliated down to her marrow; Jesus has just numbered her among the dogs, that is, with the gentiles. (There was a first-century saying among Jews: "Thank God I was not born a gentile, dog, or a woman.") The woman humbles herself: "…even the dogs eat the scraps that fall from the table of their masters." Jesus now relents: "O woman, great is your faith!" And her daughter is healed at that very moment.

For Christians, the story illustrates the power of faith and Jesus' love for all humanity. Some will see in it a Jesus undergoing a paradigm shift. The episode happened early in his ministry when his call was only to the Jews. Now he realizes his message is for everyone, Jew and non-Jew. Were Jesus beginning his ministry today, with the stranglehold political correctness has on our culture, there are those who would be labeling that early Jesus a racist (and, borrowing language from the 1970s, a male chauvinist pig, that is, a male chauvinist Jewish pig).

Actually, Matthew tells us a second time of Jesus' early ministry being meant exclusively for Jews. Matthew 10:6–7 records that Jesus sent his twelve disciples out to heal the sick and cast out unclean spirits, telling them not to go where the gentiles and Samaritans are: "But go rather to the lost sheep of the house of Israel."

When we come to the Gospel of John, chapter 4, we find Jesus pausing in Samaria, on his way from Judea to Galilee. By this time, he has extended his ministry beyond the Jews and is at ease with non-Jews. He talks to a Samaritan woman, telling her about "living water." Not much earlier he would never have stopped to talk to a Samaritan and especially a woman. That was taboo, a social no-no. However, even though his evangelistic outlook is now universal, he does remind her that "salvation is of the Jews" (John 4:22).

In Mark 5:25–34, a woman with a 12-year history of menometrorrhagia (excessive uterine bleeding during menstrual periods and other times), fearful of approaching Jesus, nevertheless gets up the courage to touch his garment: "If I may touch but his clothes, I shall be whole" (Mark 5:28). At that moment, she was indeed healed, but Jesus had a reaction to the encounter. "Who touched my clothes?" Mark's gospel states that at that instant "virtue had gone out of him" (Mk. 5:30, KJV). She thought it best to fall down before him and confess it was she, to which Jesus responded, "Daughter, thy faith hath made thee whole; go in peace." In the NKJV, "virtue" is replaced with "power" to clarify the phrase. The meaning is unambiguous in Luke 6:19 (NIV): "...and the people all tried to touch him, because power was coming from him and [healed] them all."

In any event, the Christian emphasis is on the woman's fearful state – someone in awe before the divine presence. From a Jewish perspective, Jesus as a devout Jew adhered to much of *Halakka* (the collective body of rabbinic law, custom, and tradition), especially the laws concerning impurity. Some laws we know he chose to ignore. The woman, considered a walking, bleeding, contaminating public hazard in that theocratic society, had touched him without purifying herself first. She was *tamei* [tah-may], ritually impure. "Power had gone out of him"? He would now have to undergo ritual purification by immersing himself in a mikvah (ritual bath).

I don't know how Jesus cured her. A 12-year history of heavy uterine bleeding would have left her anemic and susceptible to infections, such as tuberculosis, which apparently was widespread at the time. In an instant, he had made her whole. Hard for a scientific rationalist to figure. Well, we still can't explain how the Siberian monk Rasputin successfully treated Alexei, son of the Russian Empress Alexandria, when he had his hemophilic crises. How did Rasputin get Alexei's hematological system to muster up enough clotting factor IX to stop the bleeding into his joints? How did Jesus' power of healing manipulate the woman's physiology to stop her bleeding and also restore her to health in an instant?

CHAPTER 27

For the Japanese novelist Shusaku Endo, author of the highly regarded *A Life of Jesus*, the stern image of Jehovah in the Hebrew Bible had to be softened to appeal to the *mamasan* mentality of his countrymen. He misses the multifaceted under-standing of God the ancient Hebrews gradually acquired of Him. Nevertheless, I still admire Endo's statement that "the image of

Jesus in the Bible is a true portrait, even if it is not the Jesus of detailed fact."

Another author, Anglican priest and biblical scholar Bruce Chilton, literally manufactures an early life for Jesus that is highly speculative, as though plucked out of cyberspace. Given Chilton's scholarly credentials, his book *Rabbi Jesus: An Intimate Biography* is listed as non-fiction. On the other hand, Anne Rice, queen of the vampire novel, writes an equally speculative account of Jesus' early years, *Christ the Lord: Out of Egypt*, but her work is sold as a novel.

John Dominic Crossan, another Christian scholar,[101] describes Jesus as an illiterate Mediterranean peasant in *Jesus: A Revolutionary Biography* and elsewhere. I disagree with his assessment and will address the issue of Jesus' literacy later on.

I can go on and on in this vein, but let me mention some scholars I do appreciate and have learned from, not that the other authors mentioned have failed to teach me something as well, perhaps even a good deal. Rabbi Stephen M. Wylen's *The Jews in the Time of Jesus* is an excellent primer for anyone wanting to learn something about the first century and Jesus' place in it.

The late Rabbi David Flusser of Jerusalem is at the top of my list. Reading only one of his books, *Jesus* (no subtitle), will furnish the reader important insights into Jesus' kingdom theology, the backbone of his teaching. Likewise, *Jesus the Jewish Theologian* by

---

101 Crossan was a member of the Jesus Seminar, a group of biblical scholars who decided on the historicity of the sayings and deeds of Jesus, rating them with red, pink, grey, and black beads. At one end, a red bead meant the rater "believed Jesus did say the passage quoted, or something very much like the passage." At the other end, a black bead indicated the rater believed Jesus "did not say the passage...."

Brad Young, Flusser's Christian protégé, will introduce the reader to the role of parables in Jesus' teaching.

Old attitudes die slowly. Not too many years ago, PBS' news coverage included a segment about Jewish cadets at the Air Force Academy in Colorado being called "Christ killers." That prejudice is two thousand years old. Apparently, not everyone in the Christian world has read Pope John XXIII's prayer of 1959 asking for forgiveness: "Forgive us the curse which we unjustly laid on the Jews. Forgive us that – with our curse – we crucified Thee a second time."

Well, let me get to Jesus himself. Jesus of Nazareth, like his cousin John the Baptist, was born "in the days of Herod, King of Judea" (Luke 1:5). Herod the Great ruled from 37 till 4 BCE. So Jesus, born in Bethlehem, Judea,[102] came into the world anywhere during that 33-year span, most likely during the latter part of Herod's reign.

The year of his birth is still a sticking point. According to Matthew 2:1–16, Herod issued a decree that all male infants in Bethlehem up to the age of two years were to be put to the sword. This was his jealous and fearful response to the words of three traveling magi, probably Jewish astrologers/astronomers from Persia, who announced to him that a great king had been born in Bethlehem. Herod ordered all male infants up to the age of two years, not just newborns, born in that hamlet killed. So it's possible Jesus' birth may have occurred sometime between 6 BCE and 4 BCE.

However, there is no record anywhere in Herod's history of an infant massacre in Bethlehem during his reign. Throughout the

---

102 There was a Bethlehem in Galilee, near Nazareth, in Jesus' time. A northern Bethlehem is mentioned in the Book of Joshua 19:15, which was part of "the inheritance of the children of Zebulun."

centuries, the number of infants put to death in that tiny community grew from a couple of hundred in the early centuries to 144,000 during the Middle Ages. The Catholic Church even celebrates the event as the Feast of the Martyrs on December 28th. In all likelihood, had such a campaign of infanticide been carried out, it would not have involved more than a dozen babies, because of the limited population, and birth rate, of the village.

Once he learned of Herod's decree, Joseph took Mary and the baby Jesus and fled into Egypt, "and was there until the death of Herod…" (Mt. 2:15). Although there is no other written evidence, outside of the gospel account, of such a flight into Egypt, the apocryphal gospel literature, especially in Coptic, describes an Egyptian interlude for the family of 3–10 years. Anne Rice, in *Christ the Lord*, writes about the young Jesus in Egypt and his family's return to Galilee when he was seven. She placed their sojourn in Alexandria, which makes sense because the city had a significant Jewish population at the time. Some estimates go as high as 25 percent.

In theory, Heliopolis and Leontopolis, with their Jewish centers, would have been logical sites to have settled in as well. Leontopolis even had its own temple, built by Onias III, the ex-High Priest, who had been forced to flee Jerusalem for Egypt when removed from office by the Syrian king, Antiochus IV,[103] in 175 BCE.

If we do suppose that the family sojourned in Egypt for a number of years and were comfortable, they wouldn't necessarily have felt the need to leave immediately upon hearing the news of Herod's death. During those years young Jesus would have had time to learn Greek and Hebrew. The family, most likely, spoke

---

103 He took the title Epiphanes, meaning "the Brilliant," but the Jews referred to him as Epimanes, "the Mad One."

Aramaic at home, along with other recently arrived émigrés, whereas native Alexandrian Jews, including Philo and (his nephew) Tiberius Julius Alexander,[104] spoke Greek.

Before proceeding further, something about the nature of the Gospels should be noted. The word *gospel* means "glad tidings." It was the custom of the emperor to dispatch messengers throughout the empire whenever there was good news to share with the populace. The four canonical Gospels – Mark, Matthew, Luke, and John – are not historical documents as such, but rather accounts of incidents in the life of Jesus related in story-telling form. They cannot be compared, for instance, to the Athenian Thucydides' *The History of the Peloponnesian War*, about the war between Athens and Sparta in the fifth-century BCE. Thucydides was witness to what he wrote about. In fact, he had been a general in the war and is considered by modern historians to be a first-class historian.

CHAPTER 28

During the 1st century, there were several Jewish sects – Pharisees, Sadducees, Essenes, and Zealots – that people

---

104 An apostate Jew from a wealthy Alexandrian family, General Tiberius Alexander was Titus' second-in-command during the siege of Jerusalem in 70. At a council of war, he voted with the majority not to destroy the Temple, but during the fighting the next day, a Roman soldier threw a burning brand into a chamber of the Temple. The entire Temple was soon ablaze.

identified themselves with. Each sect claimed to have the inside track to the truth in regard to interpreting the Torah and how the priestly office should be run. They were at their height during the lifetime of Jesus and faded after the Roman destruction of the Jerusalem temple in 70 CE, which then saw the rise of rabbinic Judaism.

The most popular of these sects was the Pharisees, regularly maligned in the New Testament. The Pharisees were a significant force in the lives of the people, even though they numbered only some four thousand. They were generally respected for their knowledge of the law of Moses. What would prove crucial in the life of Jesus was the Pharisaic teaching on angels and the resurrection of the dead, beliefs not shared by the Sadducees.

The several sects were also referred to as parties and philosophies. The latter was Flavius Josephus' term for the four groups. Jesus was closest in spirit and teaching to the Pharisees, despite his verbal attacks against a handful of them: "Woe unto you, scribes and Pharisees, hypocrites!" He was singling out individuals (the Pharisaic thought police) who had been hounding him.

The Sadducees were the priestly aristocracy. They were not only pro-Roman, but they also cooperated with the foreign occupiers of the Holy Land. It goes without saying that they were not popular with the mass of Judeans and Galileans.

Unlike the Pharisees, the Sadducees did not believe in angels, those phantasmagoric creatures that first pop up in Genesis and appear throughout the Hebrew Bible and into the New Testament, nor did they believe in bodily resurrection. Jesus engages several Sadducees in a penetrating discussion on the resurrection of the dead in Mark 12: 18–25. Nor did they believe in Providence (God's intervention in the universe). For them, God was transcendent, beyond human concerns.

In the time of Jesus, the Sadducees held the power among the Jews, and they controlled the Temple. And the Roman power structure controlled the Sadducees. The high priests were generally Sadducees. Joseph Caiaphas, a Sadducean, was the high priest early in the first century, and it was this Caiaphas who would exercise a decisive role in the earthly fate of Jesus.

The Essenes were self-imposed exiles, desert ascetics, who saw themselves as the true temple priesthood. They were, however, limited geographically to the Dead Sea area, where their community at Qumran left us the famous Dead Sea Scrolls. The Essenes looked upon life as a struggle between the forces of Light and Darkness. Their leader was called the Teacher of Righteousness, who taught a century before the birth of Jesus. They despised the Jerusalem priesthood for having persecuted and killed their leader. The Essenes were apocalyptic, living, they believed, in the "end times." They would be annihilated during the Jewish-Roman War of 66–74. John the Baptist, Jesus' cousin and mentor, was, in all likelihood, an Essene at an early stage in his own short-lived career.

The 1st century Jewish historian Flavius Josephus (ne Yosef ben Matityahu) describes the Zealots as a Fourth Philosophy of Judaism. During the war against Rome, Josephus was the general who commanded the Galilean forces. Finally defeated, he saved his life by predicting to Vespasian that he would soon become emperor, which happened with the death of Nero in 69. Vespasian set Josephus up in style in Rome, where he, now as Titus Flavius Josephus, wrote his *Jewish War*, probably in Aramaic, which was then translated into Greek. Because his readership would wonder what he meant by Jewish sects but were familiar with the Greek philosophers, he called the four prominent sects "philosophies."

The Zealots began as a rebel group in 6 CE (the year of Caesar Augustus' famous census-taking proclamation that saw Joseph and

Mary travel down to Bethlehem from Nazareth to be counted (for what was really taxation purposes). Their organizer and leader was Judah (Judas) the Galilean. He was an impassioned Jew – zealous for God. It was bad enough foreigners ruled over the Jews, but the *new* tax was the final straw. The Zealots took up arms – guerrilla warfare. They were in action against the Romans on and off from then on. Two of Judas' sons would be crucified by the Romans. When full-scale war finally broke out in 66, the Zealots formed the bulk of the Jewish fighting force. Judas himself would perish in the fighting in Jerusalem.

The Zealots had their headquarters outside of Sepphoris, a major Galilean center, only a few miles from Nazareth. Joseph and Jesus probably worked in Sepphoris, which was experiencing a boom in their time. Jesus would have heard about the Zealots' exploits, perhaps even first-hand accounts of some of their skirmishes with the Romans. But the Zealots also had something to teach Jesus. If they were ferocious in their zeal for God – "No ruler but God!" was their motto – their social philosophy was one of egalitarianism, which would become one of the pillars of Jesus' kingdom theology.

After his baptism by John in the Jordan River, Jesus retired to the desert for 40 days, where, Matthew 4:1–11 tells us, he was tempted by the devil. This was now a time for soul searching. Should he join the Zealots in the struggle to free the nation from Roman occupation?

Judas the Galilean and his Zealots had been waging guerrilla warfare against the Romans since 6 CE, only to suffer heavy losses in life. Now, about the year 26, the Jewish homeland was still in bondage to Rome. Rome ruled the world, and the Zealots weren't the Maccabees (who had freed the country from Syrian control in the previous century). Armed struggle against Roman might was futile and misguided. The path to freeing his people would be as it had been in olden days – *through God's intervention.*

CHAPTER 29

Thus far I have been using the name "Jesus" to refer to the central figure in the New Testament account, and I will continue to do so. In Aramaic, it would be Yeshua; in Hebrew, Yehoshua; in English, Joshua; and in Greek/Latin, Jesus. It was customary in Hebrew for a son to be named as "the son of" so and so. Thus, we would recognize Joshua ben Joseph (Joshua son of Joseph) as Jesus. If we wish to impart a slight Aramaic flavor to his Anglicized name, we would have Joshua bar Joseph. For Catholics, Joseph was Jesus' foster father, and Jesus was solemnized as the son of the Holy Spirit.

There is a bump in the road, however. Anglican priest Bruce Chilton, in his *Rabbi Jesus: An Intimate Biography*, refers to Jesus as a *mamzer*,[105] an offspring of disputed parentage. The question is: who was Jesus' father – God as the Holy Spirit, or Joseph? For Christians, according to the New Testament, it was the Holy Spirit. For Jews and others who do not go along with the concept of immaculate conception, it would be Joseph.

Even Luke (3:23) had his doubts about Jesus' paternity. The entire verse reads: "Now Jesus himself was about thirty years old

---

105 For more on this issue, see Peter Schafer's *Jesus in the Talmud* (2007), pp. 18–24.

when he began his ministry. He was the son, so it was thought, of Joseph" (NIV). The KJV wording is: "And Jesus himself began to be about thirty years of age, being (as was supposed) the son of Joseph...." It's a rarity to encounter parentheses in the pages of the KJV.

Matthew 1:18–19 (KJV) tries to resolve the dilemma: "... When as his mother Mary was espoused to Joseph, before they came together, she was found with child of the Holy Ghost. Then Joseph her husband, being a just man, and not willing to make her a public example, was minded to put her away privily."[106] But then "an angel of the Lord appeared to him in a dream" and explained her pregnancy to him, which he accepted.

Verse 25, incidentally, states: "And [Joseph] knew her not till she had brought forth her *firstborn* [my italics] son, and he called his name Jesus." The wording of the sentence implies that Jesus was Mary's "first" son, leaving us to think there were more children. The 47 scholars who translated the Bible into English for King James I, led by John Rainolds, president of Corpus Christi College, Oxford, worked on the project from 1604 to 1611 – and those gentlemen knew their Hebrew (and Greek).

There's evidence in the Gospels that Jesus was part of a fairly large family. Matt. 13:55–56 states: "Is not this the carpenter's son? Is not his mother called Mary? and his brethren, James, and Joses,[107] and Simon, and Judas? And his sisters, are they not all with us?"

Joseph, Mary's son, isn't mentioned, and it is assumed that at this stage in Jesus' life, he is dead. The Chiltonesque view would be that if Jesus were a *mamzer*, he would quite rightly be referred to as Mary's son and not as Joshua ben Joseph. The Roman Catholic

---

106 In secret, or on the QT.
107 Joses is a shortened Greek form of Joseph.

Church maintains that Joseph had been a widower with children of his own when he married Mary.

Returning to the young Jesus, wherever he passed his childhood – Egypt or Nazareth – we next encounter him at the age of 12 years. The family was returning to Nazareth from Jerusalem, where they had gone for the Feast of the Passover. Joseph and Mary didn't realize that Jesus had been left behind until the following day, whereupon they returned to Jerusalem to look for him. On the third day, they found him in the Temple, "…sitting in the midst of the doctors, both hearing them and asking them questions. And all that heard him were astonished at his understanding and answers" (Luke 2:46–47).

His parents were relieved to find him, of course, but at the same time Mary was somewhat peeved: "…Son, why hast thou thus dealt with us? behold, thy father and I have sought thee sorrowing" (Luke 2:48). Jesus responded: "…How is it that ye sought me? Wist ye not [didn't you know?] that I must be about my Father's business?" (Luke 2:49).

Apparently, his parents didn't know. They didn't know what their young son was all about. If they had any inkling of what he was about, they would have headed straight away to the Temple, instead of searching uselessly all over Jerusalem for three days.

Years later, once he had begun his ministry, astonished townspeople would ask: "Where did he get such wisdom without having studied?" But already at the age of 12, he had demonstrated a knowledge of Torah and the Oral Law that had drawn the admiration of the elders of the Temple. Indeed, he had been studying, regardless of whatever else he had been doing.

After the Temple incident, we do not hear anything more about Jesus (except that he returned with his family to Nazareth) until the age of thirty, when he is baptized by John. Bruce Chilton, in *Rabbi Jesus*, fills in Jesus' "hidden years" by having the 12-year-old, whom he portrays as an alienated *mamzer* (and 7 years old), joining John the Baptist's group in Jerusalem as a disciple[108] instead of returning to Nazareth with his family.

Chilton's translation of Luke 2:49 is carefully nuanced: "It is necessary for me to be among those of my *Abba*," was Jesus' response to his mother. "John is the key to Jesus' crucial teenage years," he writes. Continuing to quote Chilton: "He wanted to learn a *halakkah* from John, a 'way' of living God's covenant with Israel." For the reader interested in two other non-traditional approaches to Jesus' background, I would recommend *Jesus in the Talmud* by Peter Schafer[109] and Church Father Origen's *Contra Celsum*, which preserves fragments of Celsus' early 2nd-century *Alethes Logos*.

Jesus, I tend to think, would have surprised John Dominic Crossan, who labeled him "an illiterate Mediterranean peasant." The 12-year-old in the Temple described by Luke doesn't come across as an underage illiterate Mare Nostrum peasant.[110] Luke's portrayal of the confident youngster surrounded by Jerusalem's wisest residents adds to the mystery of the budding theological superstar.

---

108 The Talmud, which describes Jesus in unflattering terms, does name a teacher he had, Yehoshua ben Perahya, not John the Baptist. The Talmud, in the words of Peter Schafer (*Jesus in the Talmud*), is the "foundation document of rabbinic Judaism in Late Antiquity," and "the defining document of those who refused to accept the new covenant [Christianity]." I do not wish to dig up old wounds at a time when Jewish-Christian healing is in a nascent stage; so this is enough for me concerning Talmudic commentary on Jesus.

109 Professor of Religion and Ronald O. Perelman Professor of Judaic Studies, Princeton University (1998–2013).

110 In the pericope of the adulteress about to be stoned (John 8:2–11), Jesus was *writing*, not doodling, in the dust on the floor of the temple. He was certainly literate.

CHAPTER 30

The leader of the Pharisees for a time during the first century BCE was the sage Shimon bar Shetah, who was a brother of Queen Salome of Judea (reigned 76–67 BCE). His pet project, which he developed with Rabbi Joshua ben Gamla, was universal education for Jewish boys (education meaning the study of Torah). The Pharisees held to the old notion of Israel as "a kingdom of priests, a holy nation." To be a priest required literacy in the Torah.

Schooling in the bar Shetah-ben Gamla tradition began at the age of five in what was called the *Bet Sefer* (elementary school). The children sat in front of their teacher all day listening to him read a passage from the Torah, which he would then translate into Aramaic and explain its contents to them. Did the students learn to read for themselves as well, or was it all rote learning, as you can still find, for instance, in rural Pakistan, where students learn the Koran by sheer memorization? Given the Pharisaic conviction that, in theory at least, every man should be literate in the manner of a priest, it does not strain the imagination to see these 1st-century BCE children actually reading from the sacred scrolls.

Bet Sefer schooling was for a period of five years, and at the age of ten, the graduates went off as apprentices for whatever their future occupation would be. Some, mainly children of the wealthy, but also a handful of gifted students who qualified for scholarships, continued on in the *Bet Midrash* (secondary school), where they studied the Oral Law and the teachings of the sages.

Perhaps Jesus had been a scholarship boy. The gospel writers lean toward the view that he was untutored, a humble man, whose words were guided by the Holy Spirit. My version is based on Shimon bar Shetah's account as recorded in the Talmud.

Rabbi Simeon ben Menasya (2nd-3rd century CE) was a staunch proponent of children's education in the study of Torah in his day. He wrote: "Even God is filled with love for him who has a son toiling in Torah." The People of the Book (*Am HaSefer*) took the Torah seriously in every past generation – some, I wish I could say many, still do.

During the Middle Ages, Jews, alone among Europeans, could claim universal literacy. By extension, it is not at all improbable that universal Jewish literacy, or at least a significant degree of literacy, flourished even in the Galilean backwater in Late Antiquity. The 19th-century Italian priest St. John Bosco (Don Bosco) educated several thousand street urchins in Turin, proving that if the will is there, you can find a way. Bar Shetah found a way in his day.

Let us return to the scene of the 12-year-old Jesus discoursing with the circle of Temple sages. Just who were they? Well, they were Pharisaic rabbis. Yes, I know the New Testament comes down hard on the Pharisees, and the gospel writers especially have them constantly at odds with Jesus. But the Pharisaic influence in Jesus' development would be pivotal in his adult life. Their belief in angels and the resurrection of the dead were core concepts that played their role as Jesus made his way toward his destiny.

Clergyman Bruce Chilton, already introduced as the author of *Rabbi Jesus*, may have his own views concerning Jesus' early life, such as having John baptize him when he was only a child, but the gospel accounts have Jesus undergoing baptism at about the age of thirty. John, we are told in Luke 3:3, "...came into all the country about Jordan, preaching the baptism of repentance for the remission of sins," and he performed this rite on Jesus who was then an adult.

In order to understand the background to John's system of ritual immersion, it is necessary to go back to a Second Temple period concept that was extremely significant in its time, ritual purity. Terms such as clean and unclean and pure and impure only succeed in approximating what was meant by ritual purity. A person or thing was either ritually pure, *tahor*, or ritually impure, *tamei* (pronounced "tah-may"). The concept of *tahor* was considered divine in nature, and to go from the state of *tamei* to the state of *tahore* was looked upon as a Godly process. Only those ritually pure, that is, *tahore*, could proceed into the sacred interior of the Jerusalem Temple.

There were various primary sources of impurity, such as unkosher food, coming in contact with a dead body, certain skin disorders, et cetera. If you became *tamei*, or unclean, then others had to avoid touching you until you underwent a cleansing process. This was done through the medium of the mikvah – immersion in a body of so-called "living water," that is, rainwater or water from a flowing stream or river. Symbolically, it was to be a reminder of the Spirit of God moving upon the face of the deep at the beginning of creation (Genesis 1:2).

At first, the ritual was limited to priests and visitors to the Temple complex. By the first century, the mikvah bath for purification had become an institution practiced everywhere. The expression, "Cleanliness is next to Godliness," originates here. Ritual purity, in the national consciousness, gradually came to mean getting close to God. If sinful acts implied distancing oneself from God, then atonement for one's sins would bring one near to God.

John the Baptist succeeded in linking ritual purification with atonement. With it came an experience of ascending to a higher level of spiritual consciousness – at least for some, Jesus for example. For Jesus, who was without sin, baptism served this particular purpose, for he "went up straightway out of the water: and, lo, the heavens were opened unto him, and he saw the Spirit of God descending like a dove, and lighting upon him: And lo a voice from heaven, saying, 'This is my beloved Son, in whom I am well pleased"' (Matt. 3:16–17). So Jesus is transformed, and now he is ready for his own mission.

We cannot determine from the gospel accounts at what age Jesus joined John the Baptist. There is a growing consensus among scholars that Jesus was indeed numbered among his disciples. How long his discipleship lasted we do not know. After his baptism, Jesus went his own way.

We read in chapter 3 of the Gospel of John, beginning with verse 22: "After these things came Jesus and his disciples into the land of Judaea; and there he tarried with them, and baptized." John and his disciples are also in the vicinity. The two groups of disciples get into an argument, and John's followers complain to their teacher: "…Rabbi, he that was with thee beyond the Jordan, to whom thou barest witness, behold, the same baptizeth, and all men come to him" (John 3:26).

Ah, a squabble between competing camps! In John the Baptist's explanation to his disciples, John of the Gospel writes: "…I said, I am not the Christ, but that I am sent before him… He must increase, but I must decrease" (John 3:28, 30). Was that really the case? Was the towering figure of John the Baptist cut down to size by the Gospel writers in order to magnify Jesus? There are scholars who think John was more than the herald of Jesus.

There is an interesting conclusion to the incident between the two rival groups of disciples. From John 4:1–2: "…Jesus made and baptized more disciples than John, (Though Jesus himself baptized not, but his disciples)" (John 4:1–2). Jesus was planning to abandon John's Essene approach of spiritual purification through water, and the confinement of the river environment, to reach out to far more people in Galilee and Judea.

Following the news that John had been imprisoned, Jesus launched his own program. Matthew 4:17 states: "From that time

Jesus began to preach, and to say, 'Repent: for the kingdom of heaven is at hand.'"

Nevertheless, despite the rivalry, John the Baptist and Jesus of Nazareth were apparently close, at least for a while, with John as teacher and Jesus as disciple. Luke 1:36 considers them relatives – Jesus' mother Mary and John's mother Elizabeth are described as cousins.

John's outlook was eschatological, apocalyptic, and messianic – part of the legacy he had acquired while with the Essenes. That last sentence contains one or more words that may require definition. Apocalyptic refers to the use of symbolic and metaphoric language to describe a future heavenly intervention. Between 200 BCE and 100 CE, there were a number of apocalyptic writings, such as 1 Enoch, Book of Jubilees, the Testaments of the Twelve Patriarchs, et cetera. The best known such work is the Book of Revelation, which begins with the Greek word *apokalupsis*, meaning "revelation." The Book of Revelation, unlike the others named above, is totally apocalyptic.

Eschatology (from Gk. *eschatos*, last + + *logos*, word) is the study or doctrine of the last days or last things. The Bible presents history as goal-directed, with God driving it from its beginning to its ultimate end.

The 1st century was a time of messianic expectations. Messiah in Hebrew [*mashiach*] means "the anointed one," as in the case of the prophet Samuel anointing Saul king of Israel and later anointing David. The Greek equivalent is *Christos*, or Christ in English. The anointed one is king.

Around the year 24 or 25 John left the Essene community and went his way out into the desert. Mark 1:4 states it simply: "John did baptize in the wilderness, and preach the baptism of repentance for the remission of sins." At some point, Jesus joined him. But there came a parting of the ways. We then find John having second thoughts about Jesus. While in prison, he sent two of his disciples to Jesus with the question, "Art thou he that should come? Or look we for another?" (Luke 7:19).

"And in that same hour [when John's emissaries arrived] he [Jesus] cured many of their infirmities and plagues, and of evil spirits; and unto many that were blind he gave sight." Luke lays it on a bit thick here – a touch of that familiar 1st-century Semitic hyperbole encountered regularly in the writings of the time.

Actually, their approaches were quite different. Jesus' style stressed love of God and love of neighbor, encapsulated in Matthew 22:37–40: "Thou shalt love the Lord thy God with all thy heart, and with all thy soul, and with all thy mind. This is the first and great commandment. And the second is like unto it, Thou shalt love thy neighbor as thyself. On these two commandments hang all the law and the prophets."

The two were proceeding in different directions. John stressed Israel's sins and the imminent judgment of God. He stuck to baptism to prepare for the Last Judgment. Jesus, on the other hand, had moved beyond baptism by water to preach about a kingdom that comes from God but before we are to face the Last Judgment. Baptism by water would be replaced by the Holy Spirit.

For John the Baptist, his wicked era – which is still here nineteen centuries later – culminates with the end of the world, and there is no intermediary period. This is John's eschatology, not Jesus'.

Jesus, as I pointed out with the experience we have of him at age 12 in the Jerusalem Temple, had some teaching at the hands of the Pharisaic sages. These were the rabbis who promulgated the concept of the kingdom of heaven. The two theologians, John and Jesus, had different eschatological timetables, and this is where they parted theological company.

In the Essene writings – and I have already alluded to John's probable Essene background – the Last Judgment closes the current history of humanity. John believed the Last Judgment was imminent. Jesus saw an additional stage of history, the kingdom of heaven, before the Last Judgment.

I tend to follow Rabbi David Flusser's explanation of the two theological giants' messianic timetables. Jesus' division of the history of salvation was tripartite, Rabbi Flusser writes in his book *Jesus*. The first, the biblical period, ended with John the Baptist. Matthew 11:13 reads: "For all the prophets and the law prophesied until John." The present period, beginning with Jesus' ministry, is the era of the kingdom of heaven. The third period, to begin at some future time, will be ushered in with the coming of the Son of Man, the almighty superhuman judge of the Last Judgment. Both systems, John's and Jesus', envisioned an end of the world and a new creation, the "age to come," and with it life indefinite.

In Matthew 3:11, John humbly states: "I indeed baptize you with water unto repentance, but he that cometh after me is mightier than I, whose shoes I am not worthy to bear: he shall baptize you with the Holy Ghost…." (Matt. 3:11). The Gospels place John in a secondary role as the precursor or forerunner to Jesus. I have already questioned this view.

The discovery of the Dead Sea Scrolls and other Jewish apocalyptic writings of the period provides evidence that John most likely had been part of one of the Essene desert communities, probably the Qumran community. He left because he was God-inspired to build a ministry based on his own eschatological Weltanschauung.

The opening of Mark's gospel has John going out into the wilderness preaching a baptism of repentance for the forgiveness of sin, reminiscent of the Essenes with their doctrine of repentance and baptism. His was a voice calling: "In the wilderness prepare," echoing Isaiah 40:3: "The voice of him that crieth in the wilderness, Prepare ye the way of the LORD...." People came from all over, even the sophisticates of Jerusalem, to be immersed in the waters of the Jordan, but more to boast that they had been baptized by John than to celebrate the meaning of the baptism. Rabbi John, the Teacher, was becoming more and more like his own inspirational figure, the Teacher of Righteousness of the Essenes, put to death more than a century earlier (150 years before the birth of Jesus).

Jesus paid honor to John: "...Among them that are born to women there hath not risen a greater than John the Baptist: notwithstanding he that is least in the kingdom of heaven is greater than he" (Matthew 11:11). An odd statement, to be sure. The next verse expands on what Jesus is getting at: "And from the days of John the Baptist until now the kingdom of heaven suffereth violence, and the violent take it by force." Instead of "suffereth violence," the KJV translation, "the kingdom of heaven has been forcefully advancing and forceful men lay hold of it," is a little easier on the eyes, but both renditions still require explanation.

John represented the end of the old covenant era, which began with Abraham; he was not part of the new period, the age of the kingdom of heaven now dawning, into which a number of bold, thoughtful men had already made their way.

Stated once again, John's thinking was shaped by the Essenes, Jesus' by the rabbis. John did not preach about the kingdom of heaven, a rabbinic concept. Jesus preached the kingdom of heaven. So how does one enter this kingdom that Jesus preached about? Luke 17:20–21 tackles the question: "...The kingdom of God cometh not with observation: Neither shall they say, Lo here! Or, lo there! For, behold, the kingdom of God is within you."

If the kingdom of God is within you, then the implication is that the kingdom is spiritual and internalized, as opposed to material and in full view of the world. If it is spiritual, you cannot see it. Jesus' aim was to make what was not visible visible, to externalize the spiritual, to bring God's heavenly kingdom down to earth.

It was not uncommon for the rabbis to boil God's 613 commandments (mitzvot) as found in the Mosaic law down into two to make a point, something Jesus picked up on. Matthew 22: 35–36 has one of the Pharisees, a lawyer, asking Jesus: "Master, which is the great commandment in the law?" Jesus, as already noted, responded by quoting Deuteronomy 6:5 and Leviticus 19:18.

The verbal exchange, which probably occurred in the courtyard of the Jerusalem Temple, continues in Mark 12:33, with the Pharisee, here called a scribe, confirming Jesus' statements and adding that these two commandments are more important than all the burnt offerings and sacrifices offered up to God. Jesus then says: "Thou art not far from the kingdom of God" (Mark 12:34).

Verbalizing these two important commandments is one thing, putting them into action, another. As Teresa of Avila would say sixteen centuries later, "It is action the Lord requires of thee." It is through actions that one gains entry into the kingdom of heaven. And for that matter, James, the brother of Jesus, who headed the Nazarene community following Jesus' death, repeats the theme when he writes that faith without works is useless, that faith must be put into action (James 2:14–26).

Now, Jesus preached about the kingdom of heaven, also referred to as the kingdom of God. Why the apparent distinction? Concerning the wording, Matthew's Gospel mentions kingdom of heaven 33 times and kingdom of God only 4 times. Mark and Luke speak of the kingdom of God. Matthew, the most Jewish of the gospel writers, was sensitive to the Jewish tradition not to invoke the divine name. Periphrastic substitution is the technical term for such word switching.

Jesus saw himself at the head of a mission to bring about a new world order of righteousness and peace, but a world in which evil would still not be wiped out. *Kingdom theology* lies at the center of Jesus' teaching. And kingdom theology was a favorite subject of the rabbis of the first century. The idea of the kingdom of heaven was peculiarly rabbinic, and Jesus embraced it, giving it his own imprimatur.

But Jesus' words on the kingdom remain somewhat obscure. The kingdom of God is already present but far from being fulfilled. It is here, and then again, it doesn't seem to be here. We long for an end to suffering and evil and for peace on earth, good will to men. However, evil will continue to exist alongside good in the kingdom of heaven, until the coming of the Son of Man. The time of the kingdom of heaven is before the coming of the Son of Man and the final judgment, followed by the resurrection of the dead. In the post-historical age that is to come, the resurrected will be a kind of new creation – somewhat in the nature of angels.

This is the third time I have had occasion to refer to the Son of Man. Some background concerning this term is indicated. We first encounter the Son of Man in the Book of Daniel, where we read about "one like a son of man coming with the clouds of heaven" (Dan. 7:13, NIV). I mentioned the Son of Man twice in this sentence, writing it first in upper case and then in lower case. In Hebrew and Greek, there is no upper case and, for that matter, no lower case, only one uniform way of writing letters. Written in lower case, "son of man" merely means a son of Adam (*ben adam*), which is any and every man. In upper case, we think of the individual in Daniel 7:13 endowed with supernatural attributes.

The term Son of Man had messianic overtones in Jesus' time. Jesus refers to himself as the "son of man" a number of times as recorded in the Gospels. When he says, "The son of man has no place to rest his head," we have no way of knowing if he is referring to himself as one of the sons of Adam or as the Messiah.

Incidentally, claiming to be the Messiah was not a crime in the eyes of the Jewish court (Sanhedrin), but was for the Roman occupiers who considered messianism a danger to their rule. There could be no king but Caesar, and talk of the Messiah was considered subversive.

In John 18:33, Pontius Pilate asks Jesus: "Art thou the king of the Jews?" A few verses later (18:36) Jesus responds: "My kingdom is not of this world." True, his kingdom will begin not in the present world but in the post-historical age that follows the final judgment. Pilate wasn't up to a deep theological discussion with Jesus and kept flitting in and out of the room.

Pilate wouldn't have understood Jesus' kingdom theology even if he had remained long enough to listen to his prisoner. The kingdom of heaven is here, although not too many people are aware that it's here. If the kingdom can be compared to a giant-sized bubble, some people are inside it, others are standing on its surface looking in but not understanding what they see, and still others, although standing on it, aren't aware of the existence of the bubble.

Jesus preached a gospel of love. His concept of universal love was an extraordinary one for the pagan world of the first century, a world characterized by brutality, power, and depravity on an unimaginable scale against a background of widespread human misery. Even his disciples found it hard to grasp his mission. Jesus had to repeat his central message to them to the very end of his life: "My command to you is this: Love one another as I have loved you."

Judas alone among the group grasped Jesus' basic teaching, but rejected it. For him, Jesus' kingdom of God with its hoped for perfected humanity was a pipe dream. People were not a lovable, trustworthy lot; the human species was incapable of rising to the level of near godliness, which was what Jesus' doctrine of love called for.

Judas was the only Judean among Jesus' Twelve; the others were Galileans like the Teacher. Judas' full name as we have it was Judas Iscariot. Iscariot may have been derived from *Sicarii*, the so-called dagger-men, who were assassins specializing in stabbing to death Roman collaborators. He also appears to have functioned as the treasurer for the group – a man of the world as opposed to Jesus' rustics from the Galilean backwater. If the script called for a betrayer, then Judas was someone sent from central casting.

Matthew 4:23 relates that "…Jesus went about all Galilee, teaching in their synagogues, and preaching the gospel of the kingdom [his kingdom theology], and healing all manner of sickness and all manner of disease among the people." Here we have the statement of Jesus' three-fold ministry: teaching, preaching, and healing.

His fame as a healer "went throughout all Syria" (Mt. 4:24): he healed those with "severe pain, the demon-possessed, those having seizures, and the paralyzed." The Greek word for "those having seizures" originally carried the meaning of moonstruck – the thinking at the time was that seizures were caused by changes in the moon.

Apparently, casting out demons was a specialty with Jesus. Demons, also referred to as evil spirits in Scripture, are fallen angels who joined Satan in his rebellion. Demonic possession can take a number of forms: muteness, deafness, blindness, seizures, supernormal strength, and self-destructive behavior, to cite a few. Whether the cause was organic or functional, to use the psychiatrist's terminology, the cure was effected through faith in the power of Jesus. However, we are not told of his failures on the road, only that he could not work any miracles in his home town of Nazareth.

When several Pharisees heard that Jesus had cured a man "possessed with a devil, blind, and dumb," their comment was: "…This fellow doth not cast out devils, but by Beelzebub the prince of the devils" (Mt. 12:24). Jesus responds: "But if I cast out devils by the Spirit of God, then the kingdom of God is come unto you" (Mt. 12:28). What Jesus is saying is that he heals through the power of God, not the King of Hell, and that is proof of his authority to preach the kingdom of heaven.

Because more than a third of Jesus' words in the synoptic Gospels are in the form of parables – a popular method of religious teaching unfolded in the form of storytelling by the rabbis of the period – an exploration of Jesus' parables will add to an understanding of his character and mission. Actually, the parable, or *mashal* in Hebrew, appears early in the Hebrew Bible. For instance, there is the parable Nathan used to confront David in 2 Samuel, chapter 12, and the parable of the trees in search of a king in the story of Gideon in the Book of Judges.

We have to bear in mind that the number of rabbinic parables was enormous, and Jesus added to and borrowed from this religious art form. The Gospel parables of Jesus, thus, are Jewish parables. Parables were the theological bread and butter of the 1st-century rabbis, and Jesus feasted on them.

Because there will be non-Jews reading this work, let me explain that the teachings of the Hebrew Bible are usually divided into two: *halakkah* and *agada*. *Halakkah*, or Jewish law, is the body of rules and practices Jews are expected to follow, such as the various biblical commandments, rabbinic pronouncements, and traditional customs. *Agada* refers to basic principles and ideas which are often taught in the form of parables and metaphors.

In other words, parables are a form of *agada* – storytelling with a higher theological meaning.

The *mashal* was delivered as a story meant to teach a particular truth, and it was worded in such a manner that its meaning would require explanation (or *nimshal* in Hebrew). For example, after Jesus – seated in a boat on the Sea of Galilee – had related the parable of the Sower to a multitude on the seashore (Mark 4:3–9), he then had to explain its meaning to his disciples, who were as much in the dark as to its meaning as were those on shore.

The *mashal* was delivered without the *nimshal* on purpose. The substance of the parable was deliberately couched in language meant to conceal its meaning. Jesus would not unravel his parable for the public, but he would for his disciples. In Matthew 13:11, Jesus says that "it is given unto you to know the mysteries of the kingdom of heaven, but to them it is not given." Matthew repeats this point a few verses later: "All these things Jesus spoke to the multitude in parables; and without a parable he did not speak to them, that it might be fulfilled which was spoke by the prophet, saying, 'I will open my mouth in parables; I will utter things kept secret from the foundation of the world'" (Mt. 13:34).

If I tear a ten dollar bill in two – a five dollar bill will serve as well – and give you only one half, that half has no value until you receive the other half from me. Jesus reserved his explanations for his disciples – they would receive both halves, the *mashal* and the *nimshal*. The *nimshal* was for those with whom he had established relationship. Discipleship was the term the 1st-century rabbis used. Those standing on the seashore that day who were truly interested could obtain understanding of the words they heard from the Teacher by becoming his disciples.

All three synoptic gospel writers include the parable of the Sower – Matthew 13:3–9, Mark 4:3–9, and Like 8:5–8 – followed by Jesus' explanation. Jesus considered this parable to be basic.

He said to the Twelve (Mark 4:13): "…know ye not this parable? And how then will ye know all parables?" Not surprisingly, the parable of the Sower is about the kingdom of heaven, as are many of his parables.

The parable of the Pearl begins with a typical opening phrase used by Jesus: "The kingdom of heaven is like…" So we have: "The kingdom of heaven is like unto a merchant man, seeking goodly pearls: Who, when he had found one pearl of great price, went and sold all that he had, and bought it" (Mt. 13:45–46).

This is one of a number of short parables, and is fairly transparent. As a pearl has great value, so does the kingdom of heaven. The price for gaining the kingdom comes high, though; our merchant, who had been searching for something of spiritual value, sold everything he had when he finally came upon the kingdom.

Jesus' Beatitudes, or "blessed sayings," are an important part of Christian theology. There are eight of them, beginning with "Blessed are the poor in spirit: For theirs is the kingdom of heaven" (Mt. 5:3), and concluding with: "Blessed are they which are persecuted for righteousness' sake: for theirs is the kingdom of heaven." The Beatitudes are the introduction to the Sermon on the Mount (Matthew 5–7), which, although delivered to a large crowd, was directed primarily at his disciples as a discourse on how they should conduct themselves.

My purpose here is not to go into a discussion of the Sermon on the Mount, but rather to draw comparisons between the Beatitudes and passages from the Dead Sea Scrolls. I'll begin with the Qumran text labeled 4Q525 – which was discovered in Qumran Cave 4 and dated to the century before Jesus' ministry – and bears the title "The Blessing of the Wise," and an alternate title, "Beatitudes"; it contains beatitudes reminiscent of those contained in the Sermon on the Mount.

For instance, Matthew 5:5 reads: "Blessed are the meek: for they shall inherit the earth." The Qumran text labeled 4Q525 (vv 2.3–6) reads in part: "Blessed is the man who attains wisdom... and in the meekness of his soul does not abhor it."

Matthew 5:8 states: "Blessed are the pure in heart: for they shall see God." Verse 2.1 of 4Q525 starts off: [Blessed is the one who speaks truth] with a pure heart." And Matthew 5:11–12: "Blessed are ye, when men shall revile you...Rejoice, and be exceeding glad...." Compare this passage with verse 2.2 of 4Q525: "Blessed are those who rejoice in it."

The passage from Qumran text 4Q521, "For He shall heal the critically wounded, He shall raise the dead, He shall bring good news to the poor...," bears similarities to what is contained in Luke 4:18: "The Spirit of the Lord...hath anointed me to preach the gospel to the poor; he hath sent me to heal the brokenhearted...."

Text 4Q246 recalls the Annunciation (the angel Gabriel's visitation to Mary to inform her of her coming pregnancy) pericope in Luke 1:30–35. And it also uses a term encountered in Luke 1:32 (and Mark 5:7) for Jesus as the "Son of the Most High."

The Sermon on the Mount has a number of expressions found only in the Essene writings at Qumran. For example, "poor in spirit" (Matthew 5:3) is found in the Qumran text entitled "The War of the Sons of Light Against the Sons of Darkness," and nowhere else. Jesus' turn-the-other cheek philosophy (in Matthew 5:38–39) is also to be found in the Essenes' "Manual of Discipline" and nowhere else.

In Matthew 5:33–37, Jesus forbids oaths, that is, oaths made in common speech but not solemn, official oaths, adding that you should not swear at all, for your word should be your bond. He may possibly have had in mind what Moses said in Numbers 30:2: "If a man...swears an oath to bind himself by some agreement, he shall not break his word; he shall do all that proceeds out of his mouth."

Then again, the inspiration for Jesus' statement on oaths may have come from the "Manual of Discipline" (vv 2.24, 26), wherein Qumran is referred to as "the community of truth," pointing out the Essenes' emphasis on truth-telling. The Jewish historian Josephus, in his *Antiquities of the Jews*, points out that the Essenes were exempt from taking the mandatory oath of loyalty to King Herod. Their word was their bond.

These similarities tend to indicate that Jesus had more than a passing familiarity with the Dead Sea Scrolls. In all likelihood, his exposure to them came through his teacher, John the Baptist. Whether Jesus had access to Essene writings while with John or acquired Essene lore through John's oral instruction is something we do not know. My contention is that Jesus did considerable reading as well as absorbing oral instruction.

Thus far, from what I have dug out from the three synoptic Gospels, I have been able to present Jesus as a teacher, preacher, and healer. The fourth Gospel, John's, does not enter into my discussion. It was written to tell the reader how to find eternal life and is an argument for the deity of Jesus, a concept alien to the Jewish mind: "Thou shalt have no other gods before me," and "Thou shalt not make unto thee any graven image, or any likeness of any thing that is in heaven above…" (Exodus 20:3–4). No Jew can worship a dead Jew. That is the lesson left us from the death of Moses, who walked off into the hills at his end so that the people would not have his body to worship.

CHAPTER 31

Two major issues concerning Jesus remain: Jesus as prophet and Messiah. The Hebrew word for prophet is *nabi*, from a verb meaning "to bubble forth," as in a fountain. A prophet is someone who pours forth or announces the word of God. Even the Greek word for prophet, *prophetes*, carries the meaning of one who speaks for another, or more specifically, one who speaks for a god. The meaning of prophet as one who also predicts future events does not enter directly into the following discussion.

In the Jewish tradition, the Age of Prophecy came to a close with Malachi near the end of the 5th century BCE. There have been no prophets since. Contrary to Jewish officialdom's position, Jesus of Nazareth and John the Baptist are for me part of the Jewish tradition. Christian theology places them with the prophets. So we have a problem. How can this dilemma be resolved?

The time of the prophets, when the Holy Spirit spoke through these specially set-aside individuals, petered out some twenty-four centuries ago. The Holy Spirit may have departed from Israel, but a heavenly voice, an echo voice of heaven, the so-called daughter voice, *bat kol* in Hebrew, replaced prophetic inspiration. The *bat kol* kept the spirit of the prophetic tradition alive, while the Holy Spirit remained silent until the time would be ripe for the renewal of prophecy. This would be initiated by a charismatic figure, such as the Messiah. Such an individual might have been Hillel the Elder (70 BCE-10 CE), so holy as to be deemed worthy for the *Shekhinah*,[111] the Holy Spirit, the presence of God in the world,

---

111 Originally, "God's presence" or "God's manifested glory." Also the dwelling place of God, especially the Temple in Jerusalem.

to rest upon him, as it did on Moses. But Hillel's generation was judged not to merit it. So says the Talmud.

Around the year 24 or 25 CE, a little less than two decades after the death of Hillel the Elder, a young rabbi left the Essene community of Qumran and began a ministry in the desert. He preached the coming of God's judgment and enjoined the people of Judea and Galilee to cleanse themselves of sin through a ritual of baptism. He would be known to us as John the Baptist, a messianic figure in his time.

Luke 1:80 introduces him: "And the child grew, and waxed strong in spirit, and was in the deserts till the day of his shewing unto Israel." ("Deserts" could refer to one of the desert communities, such as Qumran.) Continuing in Luke, verse 3:3: "And he came into all the country about Jordan, preaching the baptism of repentance for the remission of sins." Luke 3:3, by the way, sounds about the same as the Essene "Rule of the Community" 3.6–9 concerning baptism for the purpose of repentance.

John was the son of Zacharias, a Jerusalem Temple priest, and Elizabeth, a descendant of Aaron, the first priest of Israel. He was consecrated as a Nazirite (a la Samson and Samuel). During his ministry, he was looked upon as a prophet, as Elijah redivivus – Elijah brought back to life. The penultimate Torah passage closing out the Book of the Prophets, and the Age of the Prophets, Malachi 4:5, reads: "Behold, I will send you Elijah the prophet before the coming of the great and dreadful day of the LORD." The message Rabbi John would trumpet in the desert was: "The day of the LORD is near."

What can be said of John is that the people proclaimed him a prophet. He spoke with moral authority, for his was the moral voice of the people. When he accused King Herod Antipas of sin – breaking God's law – by marrying Herodias, his brother's ex-wife, the royal palace shook to its foundation. Unlike Nathan, the prophet who boldly confronted King David over his illicit affair with Bathsheba and lived to prophesy another day, John's boldness cost him his head.

The story of John's death is a familiar one, having been dramatized on stage and screen often enough. Robert Ryan as the wilderness prophet in *King of Kings* (1961) comes to mind, and also Rita Hayworth as *Salome* (1953). All the films follow the account as recorded in Mark 6:17–29. In a nutshell, Herod Antipas had married Herodias, his deceased brother's wife. "It is not lawful for thee to have thy brother's wife," John, the moral conscious of the nation, rebukes him. Herodias seethes with hatred for John, but waits for her moment to revenge herself on him. Herod protected the holy man, more out of fear, but at the same time "he liked to listen to him." On his birthday, he gives a banquet, and Herodias' daughter delights him with her dancing. He swore he would give her anything she wished for, "even half of my kingdom." The damsel, as she is referred to in the KJV, consults with her mother, and then asks for the "head of John the Baptist." Herod had sworn in the presence of his numerous guests and cannot back away. Soon enough, she is brought John's head on a platter.

John Dominic Crossan, author of *Jesus: A Revolutionary Biography*, considers this account to be a "marvelous fiction." It obscures the real reason: Herod Antipas' fear that the Baptizer's popularity threatened his crown.

It was an angel of the LORD who told Zacharias that his wife Elizabeth would bear a son to be named John, and in Luke 1:15, we are told that "he shall be filled with the Holy Ghost [Spirit], even from his mother's womb." John will be forever linked with Isaiah and Jeremiah. From Isaiah 49:1, we have, "...The LORD hath called me from the womb," and from Jeremiah 1:5, "Before I formed thee in the belly I knew thee, and before thou camest forth out of the womb I sanctified thee, and I ordained thee a prophet unto the nations."

John is the seminal figure in the apocalyptic movement of early first-century Judaism. When he left the Qumran community, he had an agenda of his own. His was a voice preaching in the wilderness: "Repent, and prepare for the Last Judgment." In John Waynian language, he was not riding point for anyone, but was leading a movement of his own.

About 150 years earlier, a group of Temple priests, fed up with the corruption of the Jerusalem priesthood, left to establish their own community in the desert. Their leader was called the Teacher of Righteousness, and he would subsequently suffer a brutal death at the hands of his former Temple colleagues. John was familiar with the life story of the Teacher, and now assumed his role, modified to his own purpose, in the world.

The Gospels would portray him as the forerunner of the younger Jesus of Nazareth, the herald who would prepare the way for the Master. What way? He was the Teacher of Righteousness, if not redivivus, then in spirit. He had marked out his own way. The Gospels describe John's baptism ritual as a baptism of repentance in preparation for the coming of the Messiah: Jesus. But John, head of his own ministry, saw his baptism rite as preparing the way for the end of this age and the coming Day of Judgment with the appearance of the Messiah: John.

However, he was put to death before he could accomplish his mission. But John was not forgotten. Acts 18:25 mentions an Alexandrian Jew named Apollos, who Paul came across in Ephesus. Apollos, the verse states, "knew only the baptism of John." Ephesus had acquired a small colony of followers of John who hadn't heard of Jesus' crucifixion as yet. In fact, John's followers had already fanned out across Asia Minor (most of today's Turkey) and into Egypt.

In the "Clementine Recognitions," writings (arbitrarily) attributed to Pope Clement 1 (papacy, 88–99 CE), John's followers assert that their Teacher had been greater than Jesus and was the true Messiah. In addition to Christianity, Islam and Mandaeanism, but not Judaism, regarded John as a prophet. The Gnostic religion of the Mandaeans, beginning back in the 1st or 2nd century, has followers to this day in southern Iraq, the Iranian province of Khuzestan, and adherents scattered abroad, numbering about 50,000 to 70,000.[112] John is considered their greatest teacher and, incidentally, Jesus and Muhammad are dismissed as false prophets.

Jesus pronounced John to be the last and greatest of the prophets. In doing so, he left himself out. But Jesus was a prophet – he spoke God's words to the people. "For I have not spoken of myself, but the Father which sent me, he gave me a commandment, what I should say, and what I should speak…whatever I speak therefore even as the Father said unto me, so I speak" (John 12:49–50). Also, from John 7:16: "My doctrine is not mine, but His that sent me." These are the words of a prophet who acknowledges the source of his message as coming directly from God.

We know from the Gospel accounts that Jesus' baptism concluded differently than John's. Luke describes the heavens opening, and then, as previously stated on page 164, "the Holy Ghost descended in a bodily shape like a dove upon him, and a voice came from heaven, which said, "Thou art my beloved Son; in thee I am well pleased" (Luke 3:21–22).[113]

---

112 Based upon data available in 2005.

113 Taken from Psalm 2:7: "I will declare the decree: the LORD hath said unto me, Thou art my Son; this day I have begotten thee." For Christians, the "thee" refers to the Anointed One (Messiah); for Jews, the psalmist has David in mind.

In the four hundred years since Malachi, the last of the prophets of the Age of Prophecy, preached, only the *bat kol*, the "daughter voice," descended on a chosen one, and that was on rare occasions, whose presence was announced by a cooing sound like that of a dove. With Jesus, God's very voice conferred the Holy Spirit on him.

For forty days and without food during his desert retreat, Jesus, now protected by the Holy Spirit (chapter 4 of Luke), resisted everything the devil could tempt him with. Having overcome that challenge, Jesus returned home and went to the synagogue on the Sabbath, where he read from Isaiah: "...The Spirit of the LORD is upon me." That day he began his public career as a teacher, preacher, healer...and prophet.

A prophet is one who speaks for God, as already explained. And the people recognized Jesus as a prophet. When he cured a blind man (John 9:17), who was then asked by several Pharisees who he thought Jesus was, the blind man responded, "He is a prophet."

In Matthew 21:45–46, we read: "Now when the chief priests and Pharisees heard his parables, they perceived he was speaking of them. But when they sought to lay hands on him, they feared the multitude, because they took him for a prophet."

Upon his triumphal entry into Jerusalem, on what is called Palm Sunday, some asked, "Who is this?" Others answered, "This is Jesus, the prophet from Nazareth of Galilee (Mt. 21:10–11).

What should no longer be overlooked or ignored by today's Jewish world is the realization that the populace in Jesus' time considered him a prophet, aware as they were that the tradition held that the Age of Prophecy had ended four hundred years earlier.

We come to the pivotal question: Was Jesus the Messiah? The answer is yes and no. If you're Christian, it's yes; if Jewish, no. What about Jesus – did he think of himself as the Messiah, or was that his followers' idea?

Let us return to the scene where the imprisoned John the Baptist sends two of his disciples to Jesus to inquire: "Art thou he that should come, or do we look for another?" Jesus avoids a direct answer and responds by referring to his numerous healings. Obliquely, Jesus has affirmed that he indeed is the one expected.

Again, in Mark 8: 27–30, Jesus and his disciples pause on the road to Caesarea Philippi. Jesus asks them, "Who do the people say that I am?" This is followed with: "And they answered, John the Baptist: but some say Elias; and others, One of the prophets." Jesus then puts the question directly to Peter, who answers, "Thou art the Messiah."

Jesus would make his case for messiahship through his healings, teaching, preaching, and magnetic personality. So extraordinary were the "miracles" of Jesus that on learning of him, Herod Antipas said (Matthew 14:1–2): "This is John the Baptist; he has risen from the dead, and therefore these powers are at work in him."

His healings are often described in the Gospels as just noted, miracles, healing wonders that carried with them messianic overtones. Mark's *Gospel*, in particular, zeroes in on Jesus' messiahship. Recognition of who he was even came from strange quarters. In Mark 1:23–27, a demoniac , one possessed of an unclean spirit, reveals Jesus' identity, referring to him as "the Holy One of God." Jesus didn't want the news of his cures to get to the ears of his enemies, especially from demon-possessed people, not the best source of testimonials.

Of the 35 or so miracles reported in the Gospels, about 20 percent of them were for people with an "unclean spirit." I have no expertise on the subject of exorcism. The *Holmes Concise Bible Dictionary* defines it as the "practice of expelling demons by means of some ritual act." Jesus' technique apparently involved silent prayer followed by a command, as in Mark 1:25: "But Jesus rebuked [the man with an unclean spirit] by saying, 'Be quiet, and come out of him!'"

Curiously, Jewish folklore retains the demon possession motif with the *dybbuk*, a restless soul or evil spirit said to gain entry into someone, setting up some form of mental illness and creating a separate personality, something akin to a multiple personality monad. Like the New Testament demon, the *dybbuk* talks through that person's mouth. This unwanted intruder can be exorcised through incantations and rituals, concluding with blasts of the shofar. *Dybbuk* tales were still popular in Poland and Russian shtetls as late as the outbreak of the First World War. Jesus was so good at exorcism, he didn't need to blow the shofar.

There is no clearly delineated distinction between the natural and the supernatural in both the Hebrew Bible and New Testament. The supernatural, with its miracles, was part of Jesus' world. Who are we to say otherwise!

Mark's approach was to keep Jesus' messiahship secret. In Mark 4:26–29, we find the only parable he recorded that does not appear in the other two synoptic Gospels, the parable of the Growing Seed. The introduction to the parable comes earlier in Mark 4:22:"For there is nothing hid, which shall not be manifested; neither was any thing kept secret, but that it should come abroad." Decipherment: The seed planted in the ground is concealed from view just as Jesus' identity was concealed until the time would be ripe.

Bear in mind, though, that messiahship in the early first century, a time of Messiah fever, was up for grabs – there were numerous claimants to the title – but in the end, the jockeying narrowed down to John and Jesus. John, the frontrunner, was seen as a threat to the established authority in Galilee, and was summarily removed. There was none among his disciples to assume his mantle, and this Essene-in-the-world's mission would wither on the vine. Even if John had a successor – as Moses had Joshua and Elijah had Elisha – Jesus had the edge over the *Bet Johanan*, the School of John. It wasn't a question of whose eschatological approach was more appealing to the people. Jesus – and his *Bet Yeshua* – just had more going for him in selling his view.

To review, in Jesus' eschatological system, the coming of the Son of Man, and with him the Last Judgment, was postponed to a future time, whereas for John the end time was at hand. Jesus, according to Rabbi David Flusser in *Jesus*, identified the Days of the Messiah – the messianic age – with the kingdom of heaven. Jesus did acknowledge that the messianic period had already begun with John the Baptist, but he was now the central figure in the kingdom movement. The messianic age would end with the coming of the Son of Man, the Messiah, and the leading candidate for the crown would be...well, who else? – Jesus.

For Christians, Jesus' kingdom movement was laid out in eschatological terms. Jews, however, see it also as a social movement. Jesus was an ethicist, and in applied social theory, an egalitarian, something that rubbed off on him from the Zealots. Some might want to call him a utopian. But he was a realist.

As much as Jesus desired a perfected humanity, he understood that during the time of the kingdom of heaven, evil would not be eradicated. At the end of that intermediary stage, when the Son of Man comes at the Last Judgment, the wicked "will go away to eternal punishment, but the righteous to eternal life" (Matthew 25:46). And the poor of the earth – "Blessed are the poor in spirit, for theirs is the kingdom of heaven" – will be heavily represented among the latter.

The world at the time of Jesus was Roman, but a good part of it was Hellenized. In Jesus' Galilee, the culture was somewhat or even largely Greek, depending on which historical accounts you read. There were 12 Greek cities within 25 miles of Nazareth. Jesus avoided them. For instance, we know he never set foot in Tiberias, located midway on the western shore of the Sea of Galilee, which replaced Sepphoris, "the jewel of the Galilee," located less than 4 miles north-northeast of Nazareth, as the capital of Galilee in the early 20s. Sepphoris was the birthplace of Mary, Jesus' mother, and, according to the Gospel of James, the home of her parents, Anne and Joachim.

Hellenization posed an assimilation danger to the ancestral tradition established by Moses. Jesus came up with strategies to counter the hedonistic influence of the gentiles, superimposed on the already existing hedonism, appropriately summarized in 2 Timothy 3:4: "…high-minded lovers of pleasure more than lovers of God." Included in Jesus' theological thinking was a teaching designed to preserve the ethical/moral tradition of the venerated Lawgiver of the past: love the LORD thy God with every sinew in your body, and treat your neighbor as you would have him treat you.

I need to deal with a critical issue before proceeding. Whether Jesus was of the House of David, as the New Testament authors portray him, is a matter for genealogists. I don't grapple with that issue here. The Jewish position is simply that Jesus was mortal at birth and a mortal when he died. His followers would gain him his immortality…and more!

In the Gospel of John 7:15, several Pharisees are amazed at Jesus' grasp of the Torah and wonder "how he gained such knowledge without having studied." The implication was that he was not a product of either the School of Hillel or the School of Shammai. The phrasing of the (Greek) text does not exclude the possibility that he may have studied with an unheralded rabbi or that he may have been self-taught. One way or another, he acquired the background of a rabbinical scholar.

The Gospels only speak of the Pharisees and Sadducees and never mention the Pharisaic schools, the *Bet Hillel* and *Bet Shammai*. The only childhood story of Jesus the Gospels recount is the Temple scene when the 12-year-old Yehoshua (Jesus' Hebrew name) engages several sages in a scholarly Torah discussion. They were probably Pharisees of the Hillel School. If we go along with the current consensus concerning the year of Jesus' birth, 6 BCE, then the Temple debate occurred about 6 CE. Hillel died in 10 CE; so his presence in Jerusalem would have been very much in evidence when the young Jesus was there.

To consider Jesus a Hillelite is not such a wild guess. The grown Jesus would borrow from Hillel. For instance, Jesus' Golden Rule – "So in everything do unto others what you would have them do to you" (Matthewe 7:12) – is Hillel's dictum modified: "Do not do unto others what you do not want done to you." Hillel and Jesus both adhered to the credo of righteousness and charity, *tzedakah* in Hebrew. They were participants in *tikkun olam*, helping to repair the world.

We are taught to love our neighbor as ourselves, which is Old Testament[114] as well as Jesus and Hillel. First we must love ourselves, for if we do not, we are incapable of loving anyone. Jesus knew the sayings of Rabbi Hillel, especially the one of his quoted most often: "If I am not for myself, who will be for me, and if I am only for myself, what am I? And if not now, when?" Jesus wasted no time in living out this dictum.

Jesus had ego strength, to use our modern terminology, which was fortified by his angels in heaven. He was able to unite himself with a suffering humanity and strive against formidable odds to improve the human condition. He was no armchair theorist but a

---

114 This is the only time I allow myself to refer to the Hebrew Bible as the Old Testament!

man of action. He was very much in the world, although he may not have been of the world. He acted in the now, unafraid that the path he had carved out for himself would lead to his death, as it had for John.

He and his band of Galileans, a motley assortment of fishermen and farmers whose provincial attire and manner immediately called attention to themselves, would be the objects of derision in Jerusalem, the center of the Jewish world. Their northern Aramaic speech sounded to the eardrums of the cultured, southern Sadducees and Pharisees like Brooklynese to a Mississippian. But the Jewish power structure took the rustic rabbi seriously. He was persona non grata, and they feared the potential influence among the people of this towering spiritual giant from the sticks.

Jesus' ministry was a road show. Unlike Hillel and Shammai with their established schools in Jerusalem, Jesus and his disciples were peripatetic, constantly on the move from village to village, except for those times Jesus took respite in Peter's home in Capernaum by the Sea of Galilee. We tend to overlook the strenuousness of his labors. For instance, on one occasion his disciples panicked in their boat when the waves raged on the Sea of Galilee, while Jesus slept through it all and had to be roused from his deep slumber. His various activities that day had left him exhausted!

Jesus taught his disciples how to heal – healing was a vital part of his ministry. Matthew 10:1 words it thusly: "And when he had called unto him his twelve disciples, he gave them power against unclean spirits, to cast them out, and to heal all manner of sickness and all manner of disease." Matthew elaborates a bit in 10:8: "Heal the sick, cleanse the lepers, raise the dead, cast out devils: freely ye have received, freely give." In 10:7, he says: "And as you go, preach, saying, The kingdom of heaven is at hand." Today's public relations experts would applaud his technique.

Jesus healed even on the Sabbath in violation of the Law, which prohibited work of any kind on God's day. In Mark 2: 27–28, he rebukes his critics: "The Sabbath was made for man, not man for the Sabbath." The statement wasn't an original one.

During the Maccabean revolt against the Syrian Antiochus in the second century BCE, the devout contingent in Mattathias' army would not fight on the Sabbath, preferring martyrdom to profaning the LORD's day. The Maccabees came up with a new interpretation of the Torah on this issue: they would not attack the Syrians on the Sabbath but would fight to save their lives (1 Maccabees 2:40–41). Thus, to break Sabbath ritual in order to save a life became legitimized and would later be included in the Talmud as: "The Sabbath was made for man, and not man for the Sabbath," words Jesus would use against the Pharisees two centuries after the Maccabees.

Jesus also outraged his critics by forgiving sins, a crucial element in his healing technique. Because so much illness was associated with sin at the time, to remove sin from the picture would insure a better chance for a permanent, not just temporary, cure. In Mark 2:5, he cures a paralytic in Capernaum and tells him his sins are forgiven. This leads to an angry outcry: "Who can forgive sins but God alone?"

Yet Jesus was not alone with his healing approach. Both the Book of Daniel and the Qumran literature contain the prayer of Nabonidus.[115] Nabonidus, the last king of the Neo-Babylonian Empire (reigned from 556–539), was ill for seven years "until I prayed to the most high God [of Israel]. And an exorcist pardoned my sins. He was a Jew from among the children of the exile of Judah."

---

115 Usually confused with Nebuchadnezzar.

But Jesus always acknowledges that it is God who does the healing. In Luke 11:20, he says that he drives out demons "by the finger of God." The Ten Commandments were inscribed in stone "by the finger of God" (Exodus 31:18). When Pharaoh's magicians couldn't duplicate the plague of gnats Moses had caused by having Aaron touch the dust of the ground with his rod (Ex. 8:18), the magicians exclaimed: "This is the finger of God." The finger of God is a colorful metaphor for the power of God. Here it is used as the instrument by which God transmits His healing energy into the very marrow of Jesus.

Again and again in the Gospels, we find the Pharisees wanting to get Jesus out of the way. As an example, when Jesus cures a man with a shriveled hand on the Sabbath, "the Pharisees went out and began to plot with the Herodians[116] how they might kill Jesus" (Mark 3:6). The New Testament does not distinguish between the two divisions of Pharisees, the Hillelites and the Shammaites. Jesus never attacked Pharisaism itself, which was his theological grounding but rather those Pharisees, small numbers of Shammaites, he labeled hypocrites.[117]

It wasn't only the "Pharisees" who attacked Jesus. The majority of the populace, theologically straight-laced Jews living in a rigid theocracy, were against him, and various statements of his in the Gospels led to clashes between Jews and Jesus' adherents. Consider, for example, Matthew 5:13, Jesus' pep talk to his followers contained in his Sermon on the Mount: "Ye are the salt of the earth: but if the salt have lost his savour, wherewith shall it be

---

116 A cadre of Hellenistic Jews who hated Jesus. Little else is known about them.

117 The Shammaites were literal interpreters of the Mosaic law, whereas the Hillelites allowed for a liberal interpretation.

salted? It is thenceforth good for nothing, but to be cast out, and to be trodden under foot of men."

Uplifting words for Christians, to be sure, but now reconsider the passage from a 1st-century Jewish perspective. The Roman occupation is oppressive, and the break-away Jesus movement is gaining adherents. "The Jews," to use one of John's favorite expressions in his Gospel,[118] are not a happy lot. Matthew 5:13 reflects the changing scene. What he is actually saying is: We, the New Jews, Christ followers [soon to be called Christians and divorced from you old Jews], are now the salt of the earth. As for the Jews as a whole, they have lost their saltiness, that is, their taste, or timeliness. As such those of the old covenant are no longer "good for anything" and are to be thrown out and squashed under foot like cockroaches. Definitely, there was bad blood and acting out between those who adhered to the old covenant and those who embraced the new covenant![119]

CHAPTER 32

We actually know only a fraction of what passed between Jesus and his disciples as they went along their way. Jesus did not have a Boswell, and a mountain of words from the lips of

118 As though he had never been one! The expression, "the Jews," is used 71 times in John's Gospel.

119 This, in essence, is Peter Schafer's interpretation of Matthew 5:13 in his *Jesus in the Talmud*, pp. 23–24.

the Teacher has been lost to us. We understand there were private teachings. For instance, in the Gospel of Philip, one of the non-canonical gospels, the "guys" are jealous that Mary Magdalene may have received a special teaching from the Master.

John states the case well at the conclusion of his Gospel (John 21:25): "And there are also many other things which Jesus did, the which, if they should be written every one, I suppose that even the world itself could not contain the books that should be written."

John's hyperbole is not out of place. There is so much we don't know about Jesus, but the Christian position, theologically sound, is that God has given the world all it needs to know about him. The rest is faith, and faith involves living with unanswered questions.

Earlier I applied the term magnetic personality to Jesus. I think charismatic would also be appropriate. In 1922, the eminent German sociologist Max Weber was looking for a word to describe Othniel, the first judge of Israel (Judges 3:9), who freed the Israelites from the yoke of the king of Aram-Naharaim in Mesopotamia. Othniel was a mighty man of old, a deliverer, and a more precise word was needed to categorize this special man. Weber turned to the Greek *charisma*, meaning "gift," or "divine favor." Othniel was a gift from God to Israel. In the first century, when Israel was under Roman rule, God sent His people a charisma, Jesus of Nazareth. In Christianity, the term means an extraordinary power granted by the Holy Spirit, such as the ability to perform miracles.

Another charismatic figure just before the time of Jesus was Honi the Circle-maker (Honi ha-Me'agel), a miracle-working preacher and rainmaker. There is a lengthy harvest festival, Sukkot (Feast of Booths), which begins four days after Yom Kippur. The highlight, the recitation of the prayer for rain, comes on the eighth day, and marks the beginning of the rainy season in Israel. If Sukkot should come and go without rain, then the people would turn to prayer and fasting two days out of the week until it did rain. One year it didn't rain, and the people implored Honi to ask God for rain. He prayed, standing within a circle he had drawn, and God sent the rain.

Honi, through this miraculous act and others similar to it, incurred the jealousy of Rabbi Shimon bar Shetah, the head of the Sanhedrin (the Jewish Council). Shetah wanted to excommunicate him, but didn't dare because: "The One who is everywhere treats [him] like a son who ingratiates himself with his father, who then grants him every wish." Honi was, like Jesus, said to be without sin, and like the Nazarene referred to God on intimate terms as *Abba* in Aramaic, the equivalent of "Daddy."

Rabbi Wylen, in *The Jews in the Time of Jesus*, points out the similarity of the conflict between Shimon bar Shetah and Honi and that between the Pharisees and Jesus in the New Testament. It was the age-old conflict "between charismatic authority and traditional authority."

Honi's grandson, Abba Hilkiah, in the family tradition a rain-maker, was recognized for his humility and charity. Like, Jesus, he never claimed any glory for himself and attributed his miracles to the "Father."

Hanan ha-Nehbi, another of Honi's grandsons, was the favorite of schoolchildren. The elders would send them to him to bring the rain. They would dance around him, singing, "*Abba, Abba*, give us rain." When ha-Nehbi prayed, the rain would come.

There was a fourth charismatic miracle-worker, not a rabbi such as the others, Hanina ben Dosa, about whom many healing and miracle stories are told. One time a renowned rabbi sent for him to pray for his sick son. Hanina obliged the rabbi, and as he was leaving, said, "Go upstairs, for the child's fever has broken." Later it was discovered that the child had become well exactly at the moment when Hanina had spoken and not before. John

4:46–54 describes a similar story of Jesus healing someone from a distance, a royal official's son. Another version has him curing a centurion's servant in the same way (Mt. 8:5). And there is the episode of the Canaanite woman's daughter recounted earlier in these pages.

The charismatic miracle-workers of the Talmud had much in common with Jesus. They were said to be sinless, had an intimate father-son relationship with God referring to Him as *Abba*, experienced conflict with the established power structure, and enjoyed an unusual rapport with the people. Together with Jesus, they make up the "Abba Five," as I call them.

With the exception of Jesus, the four – Honi, his two grandsons, and Hanina – were rain makers. Rabbi Wylen points out that in ancient Israel rain was a symbol of salvation and redemption. He adds that the rabbis believed God had a special dew reserved for the end-time with which He would bring about the resurrection of the dead. Thus the "Fab Four" and Jesus were salvational figures. (They are the Pietists mentioned earlier.)

I have been asked on more than one occasion to boil Jesus' kingdom theology down to one sentence, and my response has been, "May God's reign soon prevail, in our own day, our own lives, and the life of all Israel." Actually, this turns out to be a passage in one of the pages of the Yom Kippur evening service. Furthermore, it's part of the *Kaddish*, a doxology (statement of faith) and the mourner's prayer recited regularly at Jewish services.

I asked a rabbi about the antiquity of the *Kaddish*. He said it dates back to the first century and perhaps earlier: "No one knows the original, the ur-text; it's lost in the past." After a pause, aware of my interest in Jesus, he added, "The *Kaddish* prayer is often compared to the Lord's Prayer – and that's coming from Christian theologians."

The opening words of the *Kaddish* (written in Aramaic, not Hebrew) read: "Magnified and sanctified be His great name throughout the world which He has created according to His will." Jesus strove to spread God's name throughout the world. It was a wish as old as Solomon, who invited non-Jews to come and pray in the Temple he built: "Thus all the peoples of the earth will know Your name and revere You..." (1 Kings 8:43). This is what Jesus, a thousand years later, had in mind in the way of evangelization.[120] The *Kaddish*, with its praise and glory of God and hope for the establishment of His kingdom on earth, brings us to Jesus' kingdom theology.

The third line of the Lord's Prayer (the entire prayer is in Matthew 6:9–13) is a concise statement of Jesus' kingdom theology: "Thy kingdom come, Thy will be done on earth as it is in heaven." The Lord's Prayer, it should be noted, is very much a Jewish prayer, one that I pray every morning – along with the *Sh'ma*.

In the Gospels, we encounter a Jesus frequently in prayer. What was he praying? Jesus was part of the eternal Jewish experience and would certainly pray the *Sh'ma* – "*Sh'ma Yisra'el, Adonai Eloheinu, Adonai Ekhhad* – "Hear, O Israel, the LORD is our God, the LORD is One" (Deuteronomy 6:4). These six words are Judaism's credo.

Jesus would have prayed the *Sh'ma* a minimum of four times a day, twice during the morning prayer, again in the evening, and before going to bed. Nor would he have stopped with just praying the *Sh'ma*, but would have continued with designated prayers from Deuteronomy and Numbers. In fact, after his spoken final words on the cross, "It is finished" (John 19:30), he would have died with

---

120 As expressed in Matthew 28:16–20, the Great Commission: Jesus' call to his disciples to baptize all nations in the name of the Father, the Son, and the Holy Spirit.

the *Sh'ma* on his lips, as all Jews are enjoined to pray when they know their moments of life are slipping away.

The death of Jesus by crucifixion brings to an end the story of Jesus the Jew. What followed, his resurrection, is the beginning of the story of the Christianized Jesus, but that belongs to another religion, not to Judaism.

EPILOGUE

God chose Moses to deliver His people out of bondage in Egypt and to lead them on what would be a perilous journey[121] to a sacred mountain in the land of Midian. There, on the slopes of Mount Sinai, Moses began the task of molding a henotheist/polytheist people into monotheists, a process that would take a thousand years. Little by little the Israelites were transformed into a nation, as they slowly shed alien gods and came to recognize the universality of their god, the LORD God.

That understanding came slowly. King Solomon, in the 10th century BCE, invited all the peoples of the earth to come to his temple in Jerusalem to get to know the god of Israel. The world was full of gods, but Solomon thought his god was special and wanted everyone to know it.

At the end of the 8th century BCE, Sennacherib, the mighty king of the Assyrians, was knocking at the gates of Jerusalem, but

---

121 A detailed account of the Exodus path Moses followed can be found in Colin Humphreys' *The Miracles of Exodus*.

the god of the Jews delivered them. (YHVH preserved the presence of the Jews in the world by sending Pharaoh Shabaka to aid Hezekiah.) He was still a territorial god, but now He had status and clout. An understanding of who He is was slowly evolving.

During the post-exilic period, perhaps in the late 5th or early 4th century BCE, an unknown writer wrote the story of Jonah, which he set in the time of King Jeroboam ll (8th century BCE). It took him some time to realize that Yahveh was indeed God, the one-and-only God, who sent His prophet Jonah into, of all places, the land of Nimrod to preach His message. Why go into Assyria, home of hostile pagans? Why not? After all, He – Yahveh, YHVH, I AM – was the God of All Places. And that is the ultimate meaning of the Book of Jonah.

Finally the message of Deutero-Isaiah, who wrote chapters 40–55 in the Book of Isaiah during the Babylonian Exile (6th century BCE), had substance. In Isaiah 44:6, he sounded the definitive statement of monotheism, one thousand years in development: "I am the first, and I am the last; and beside me there is no God." Judaism as a religion, the first religion, begins with the statement in Isaiah 44:6.

FINIS

CPSIA information can be obtained
at www.ICGtesting.com
Printed in the USA
FFHW021841010119
50017877-54780FF